PENGU

Annual and Biennial Flowers

A. P. BALFOUR

The object of this book is to present to the average gardener a picture of the place of annual and biennial flowering plants in present-day gardening. Full practical instruction on the best methods of growing plants from seed and raising seedlings both in the open and under glass are given. The cultivation of annuals and biennials in the average garden managed by the owner and their use to the best advantage, are also fully discussed. How new varieties arise and how the seeker after new plants goes about his work are described in another chapter. The growing of annuals and biennials for decorating the cool greenhouse and for use in the home is fully described with detailed lists of plants to use, sowing dates, times of flowering, and other useful information. Sections are devoted to each of twenty-five most widely grown annuals and biennials describing the history of the original plant and giving the range of varieties of each plant. A full descriptive list follows of all the best annuals and biennials for use in our gardens today with the exception of the twenty-five dealt with separately.

The book is full illustrated with nearly 150 plates, showing the plants and their growth and many of the principal gardening operations such as sowing, pricking out, and thinning.

Produced in conjunction and collaboration with The Royal Horticultural Society.

General Editor: Patrick M. Synge.

The illustration on the cover is of Arctotis Sutton's Special Hybrids

A vase of Annuals.

A. P. BALFOUR

ANNUAL
AND BIENNIAL
FLOWERS

*Prepared in conjunction and collaboration
with The Royal Horticultural Society*

PENGUIN BOOKS

Penguin Books Ltd, Harmondsworth, Middlesex
U.S.A.: Penguin Books Inc., 3300 Clipper Mill Road, Baltimore 11, Md
AUSTRALIA: Penguin Books Pty Ltd, 762 Whitehorse Road,
Mitcham, Victoria

—

First published 1959

—

Made and printed in Great Britain by
Jarrold & Sons Ltd, Norwich

Contents

List of Plates

8

9

10

Preface

I must thank the President and Council of The Royal Horticultural Society for the honour they have done me in inviting me to write one of the first of this series of publications. I have attempted to deal with the subject from the point of the owner-gardener.

I would not have ventured to undertake this work had it not been for the promised help of Mr Patrick Synge, whose assistance and encouragement have proved invaluable.

I should also like to acknowledge a deep debt of gratitude to Professor C. D. Darlington for his great assistance in many ways, particularly in Chapter 4, to Dr A. G. Erith of Reading University, who has helped and guided me throughout, and to Mr John Gilmour for his advice on problems of nomenclature.

I am also indebted to the kindness and generosity of Messrs Sutton & Sons in presenting so many of the illustrations and to Mr J. E. Downward whose skill and patience in the difficult art of photographing flowering plants in the open are so well known.

A. P. BALFOUR

Introduction

The general design, trees, lawns, hedges, and other permanent features are naturally of fundamental importance in every garden. Nevertheless the addition of annual and biennial flowering plants, correctly used and well grown, will add immeasurably to the decorative value of most gardens, large or small. Many of these plants are unsurpassed for their length of flowering, brilliant colouring, ease of cultivation, and general adaptability, and they frequently possess great fragrance, that quality so valuable, especially in a small garden.

The uses of annuals and biennials are many and varied. They may be grown in beds and borders by themselves or with perennial plants in mixed borders, where they increase the beauty and prolong the flowering time. They may be planted among shrubs in open woodland glades or used purely to provide cut flowers for the house. They are most valuable in the cool greenhouse and give brightly coloured and easily grown plants in pots, with a succession of flowers practically all the year round. For a garden of short tenancy, or until a more permanent lay-out can be undertaken, annuals are invaluable for filling the gap. Numerous climbing plants found among annuals are useful for covering trellis-work, old tree stumps, rough banks and fences; and even in the rock garden, annuals, if selected with care, can be a definite asset.

In general annuals prefer an open situation with air and light and to give of their best should have a well-cultivated soil with sufficient lime to make it non-acid. If it is acid, lime should be added. Visitors to Scotland are often astonished at the brilliant colour and profusion of bloom of annuals and this gives us a clue to their cultural requirements. Annuals on the whole flourish in cool moist conditions in their early stages, followed by bright warm sunshine, to produce their best. By the very fact of their having only one short season in which to complete their growth, annuals should have as good conditions of growth as possible. Careful attention to their not very exacting requirements is well rewarded.

In describing groups of plants, it has not been thought desirable to give detailed lists of varieties available. The general garden development of the plant is indicated however, and the range of variations so far obtained. By the nature of things the varieties change and are being

13

continually superseded by improved garden forms – hence the reason for the periodic trials of The Royal Horticultural Society at Wisley. To find the latest and best garden varieties available, the catalogue of a reliable seed firm should be consulted.

With regard to the use of such 'category-terms' as race, strain, group, etc., it has been difficult to follow a consistent plan throughout the book, as the present practice among growers is by no means fixed or uniform. The recently published *International Code for the Nomenclature of Cultivated Plants* has taken a first step towards rationalization, but it will no doubt be some time before all the various types of unit can be adequately covered. In many groups of annuals the genetical origin and exact status of the group is very complicated and sometimes not fully known.

1 · Cultivation

For garden purposes an annual is a plant which is sown, blooms, and dies in one year. A biennial must be sown one year and will bloom the following year.

For the purposes of cultivation, annuals may be considered under three headings.

HARDY ANNUALS, which may be sown in spring in the open ground where they are to flower.

HALF-HARDY ANNUALS, which require to be sown under glass and planted out when danger of frost is over.

TENDER ANNUALS, which are raised, grown, and flowered in pots under glass.

Hardy Annuals

SITE. For the cultivation of hardy annuals the site must be selected with care. *Annuals require light and air, and they will not succeed in dense shade or under the drip of trees.*

SOIL. They prefer a medium well-drained loam. Should the soil be on the heavy side, much can be done to make it more suitable.

LIME. Should the soil be found to be deficient in lime regular liming can be a most useful aid to cultivation. Lime could, with advantage, be applied every two or three years. Besides being a plant-food in itself, lime acts on the soil physically by causing the fine particles to coagulate together, thereby giving a better 'crumb' for the seed bed. The slug population will also be considerably reduced. Lime should always be applied to the surface of the soil, as it is soluble in water and tends to be washed down by heavy rain. Therefore, a convenient time to apply lime for annuals is a week or so before sowing, when preparing the seed bed. Another good time is when preparing land for planting, a few days before planting out. The addition of compost, strawy manure, or in fact any organic material, is also useful in making such a soil more friable and thus more suitable for annuals.

GREEN MANURING. In certain circumstances green manuring may be a great help. Sow a crop of strong growing plants such as mustard, annual vetches, lupins, and so on, in late summer, and dig in when in full growth. This helps to break up heavy soil and adds valuable humus, the decayed organic material which adds so much to the fertility of the soil.

LIGHT HUNGRY SOILS. Should the soil be too light, the addition of compost, peat, or well-decayed manure helps greatly by creating humus. In this case take care to move the soil as little as possible in the spring to prevent the loss of soil moisture. In the drier parts of England unnecessary turning up of the soil may make the difference between success and failure.

PREPARATION OF SOIL FOR SOWING. The real beginning of the gardening year is in October and then it is that the preparation for the growing of hardy annuals should be begun.

First, thorough and deep cultivation of the soil in early autumn, whether by digging or mechanized cultivation, is of prime importance. At the same time manure, preferably well-decayed farmyard or compost, should be applied. It should be kept in mind, however, that annuals flower best in not too rich a soil. If planted in over-manured soil they may tend to go to leaf rather than flower. The land should be turned up rough so that winter rains and frosts can act upon the surface (Pl. 1a) and allow it to be broken down in the spring to a fine tilth for seed sowing.

As soon as the weather becomes genial in the spring and when the soil is working freely, the surface of the soil should be thoroughly cultivated and broken down. This operation of breaking down the soil to a depth of say 3 to 4 in. must be done thoroughly (Pl. 1b). It is essential for successful results that the land is thoroughly worked and the surface made firm. In nature when annual plants shed their seeds the soil is thoroughly consolidated and firmed by winter rains and weather. In the case of very light soils, and particularly in dry weather, it will be necessary

(a)

(b)

(c)

1. Preparation of the soil. (*a*) The soil should be turned up rough and left for winter rains and frost to act on it. (See p. 16.) (*b*) Breaking down the surface by raking. The larger stones should be raked off the seed bed. (See p. 16.) (*c*) The surface must be made firm by treading, especially in the case of light soils.

to make the surface firm by treading or rolling (Pl. 1c). There must be no hollows anywhere underneath, so that on germinating the young roots can go straight down and come into intimate contact with the particles of soil. These roots, besides needing moisture, also require air; therefore the soil should not be worked when too wet and sticky as this may cause packing and thus seal off contact with the air.

THE TIME TO SOW. For seeds to germinate three things are required: moisture, air, and warmth. To get the best results the soil must be friable so that the air can penetrate to the germinating seeds. When the surface is caked, through working the soil when wet, the young germinating seedlings may actually be killed through lack of ventilation.

It is also useless to sow seed when the land is still too cold. For all seeds there is an optimum temperature for germination, varying according to the hardiness of the individual species. There is also an optimum date for sowing but this date can only be roughly gauged according to the calendar and it is far better to wait, should the season be a late one and the soil not yet warmed up. An even distribution of moisture must be maintained in the seed bed. If it is hollow, undue drying occurs and germination is inhibited, so careful consolidation and treading is necessary. The best time to sow in the spring depends, then, on conditions of temperature and moisture. Seeds are living things, weather is variable, it is therefore impossible to give exact dates for sowing; practice must be adapted to varying conditions.

METHOD OF SOWING. The best method for sowing most seeds is probably in drills made with a line and the corner of a draw hoe or the back of a rake, the depth to be varied according to the size of the seed. Having the seedlings in lines enables them to be thinned and weeded easily and the hoe should be used to keep a tilth on the land round them and keep down weeds until the young plants are large enough to cover the ground themselves.

The seeds must on no account be buried too deeply. Some very small seeds should barely be covered by the soil and can be sown

18

on the surface in showery weather and simply raked in. Large seeds must be sown more deeply so that they will receive sufficient moisture for germination, but on the other hand not so deeply as to exclude air. A good rule is to sow at a depth twice the diameter of the seed.

If the soil is really heavy and full of clay, and tends to set hard under watering in dry weather, various aids can be given to assist the seed to germinate. They should be sown in a very shallow drill which has been thoroughly soaked. After sowing cover with a light compost free from weed seeds. Another method is to cover the seed bed with sacking and to water through the sacking until the seed germinates. Take particular care to remove the sacking immediately the seeds begin to germinate, otherwise the seedlings will quickly become drawn and spoilt.

It is essential to sow the seed thinly to enable the seedlings to have room to develop and to give room for early thinning. Few things are more inimical to the successful growing of annuals than over-crowded seedlings. It is, of course, important to sow enough seed to ensure an even covering of plants but if the seed bed is correctly prepared and the soil is in good condition good germination will result. A very good method of ensuring even sowing is to decide before you start what amount of seed will be required for a given length of drill, then place it in a saucer or in the palm of the hand and distribute it evenly along the drill by finger and thumb. Another method is to mix the seed with fine dry sand.

THINNING OF SEEDLINGS. Thinning consists of two operations, the first, a preliminary thinning, should be done immediately the seedlings have germinated and are large enough to handle (Pl. 2). The final thinning should be done a week or so later, according to the development of the seedlings. The distance between the seedlings after the final thinning should be determined by the height to which the plant grows and its habit and bushiness of growth, the important factor being that each plant should have sufficient room to develop fully. All plants vary in their habit. Calendula, if thinned to 6–9 in. apart will form a bushy branching plant covered in flowers. A more slender growing annual on the other hand, such as viscaria or virginian stock,

2. Preliminary thinning. A second thinning will be required later.

prefers the support of neighbouring plants and need only be thinned to a few inches. Each plant, however, should have room to develop as an individual.

AUTUMN SOWING. Many quite hardy annuals, especially in the southern parts of England, produce larger plants and earlier and finer flowers when they are sown where they are to flower in autumn. This can be done at any time when conditions are favourable, from the end of August into September in an open, airy, well-drained position. The aim should be to arrange the times of sowing so that the resulting seedlings form bushy little plants 2–3 in. high, with root systems large enough to prevent the plants being lifted by alternating frosts and thaws but not too large to be 'winter proud' (in other words, sappy and liable to be killed by frost).

3. Bushy stakes inserted into a bed of young cornflower seedlings. Often it will not be necessary to insert twigs as thickly as this.

It sometimes happens in the south of England that the land at the end of August is bone dry and as hard as a rock, and if one attempts to fork it up it simply goes into hard intractable lumps. If this is so, and especially if the soil tends to be on the heavy side, on no account attempt to break it up but remove weeds and cultivate the surface only, working it down to a fine tilth of 2–3 in. This is quite sufficient for a seed bed and as soon as the rain comes, the seed will germinate immediately. Provided the land is in good condition, the plants will grow and flower perfectly.

EARLY STAKING OF YOUNG SEEDLINGS. Wherever they may be grown, careful and early attention to staking of the young plants is essential. At the first opportunity after final thinning twiggy sticks should be placed among the plants, stuck firmly in the ground and the height arranged so that the plants, when fully grown, will grow above their supports. This is probably the ideal method, but short bamboo canes with green raffia can also be satisfactory, if skilfully used so that the plant is allowed full development and the supports are eventually completely hidden.

REMOVAL OF DEAD FLOWERS. Another point to be noted is the removal of dead flowers and seed pods as they form. This is of the utmost importance for lengthening the period of flowering.

Half-hardy Annuals

Half-hardy annuals usually include those plants which require a longer season of growth than is supplied by our normal summers, or will not stand even slight frosts in the seedling stage. The principles of raising and sowing are really the same as for hardy annuals except that they must be sown in a frame or greenhouse from which frost can be excluded.

PREPARATION OF SOIL AND CONTAINERS FOR SOWING. The soil or compost should be light and friable and easily worked. The John Innes Seed Compost is admirable for the purpose and it is best to use sterilized soil. The John Innes Seed Compost consists of two parts medium loam, one part good peat, one part coarse sand, by loose bulk. To each bushel of this mixture add ¾ oz. ground chalk or limestone and 1½ oz. superphosphate. These quantities should be measured and the fertilizer weighed.

The most effective method of soil sterilization is by means of steam. For small quantities a 2 per cent solution of Formalin or Commercial Formaldehyde may be used. For full particulars see *Seed and Potting Composts* by Lawrence and Newell, or the leaflet published by the John Innes Horticultural Institution, Bayfordbury, near Hertford, Herts. There is also a simple electrical soil sterilizer, suitable for small gardens.

The containers, whether earthen pots or pans or wooden seed trays should be thoroughly cleaned, washed, and sterilized before being used. They must be filled evenly when the compost is 'working' well, that is, just damp enough but not so damp that it will remain sticking together in lumps when worked. It is most important to use ample drainage (Pl.4a). Some hours before sowing, thoroughly water the soil and allow the surplus to drain away properly before sowing. This should provide sufficient moisture to ensure the germination of most small seeds.

4(a)

4. Sowing half-hardy annuals in boxes. (a) Putting in the drainage material, the crocks are placed along the cracks in the base of the box and above it is placed some coarser peaty material.

4(*b*). The compost must be pressed down firmly and evenly while filling the boxes.

4(*c*). Levelling and firming the surface before sowing. A piece of flat wood with a handle attached is most useful for this.

4(*d*). The seeds should be sown thinly. These are pot marigolds.

4(*e*). Lightly cover the seeds by sifting on the compost.

25

SOWING. Sow the seed thinly and if it is very fine sow on the surface and simply press it into the soil with a flat piece of wood conveniently shaped for the purpose. In the case of tiny dark seeds, a convenient way of ensuring even and thin sowing is to cover the surface with a light sprinkling of silver sand upon which the dark seeds can be seen easily (Pl. 5a). Other seeds should be lightly covered by sifting the compost through a fine sieve direct on the seed pan or tray. Cover with a piece of glass to ensure a moist atmosphere but turn the glass over each day to prevent too much condensation. Place a sheet of paper over the glass to protect from the direct rays of the sun (Pl. 5d). When using large quantities, covering the seed trays by sheets of brown paper alone in order to save time and labour may be sufficient. Immediately the seedlings begin to appear, the covering should be removed and air given. This, together with abundant drainage and thin, even sowing, should be sufficient to avoid attack by the dreaded 'damping-off fungus'.

5(a)

5. Sowing fine seed of half-hardy annuals in pans. (a) Mixing the seed in the envelope with silver sand to ensure even distribution over the pan. (b) Sowing the seed. (c) Plunging the pans after sowing in a bath of water. The level of the water should be below the rim of the pan. (d) Cover the pans with panes of glass and place newspaper over the glass to shade from the sun.

5(b)

5(c)

5(d)

27

6. Young antirrhinum seedlings showing effect of 'damping-off' fungus.

'DAMPING-OFF' FUNGUS. This fungus appears when the surface of the seed pan is allowed to remain too wet as a result of insufficient drainage. The fungus grows on the surface of the soil and penetrates the neck of the young seedling just where it emerges from the soil, causing it to fall over (Pl. 6). This can easily be observed under a low-powered lens. Under favourable conditions this fungus spreads very quickly, causing irregular patches over the seed bed, and will rapidly destroy all the seedlings unless checked.

In the case of seeds which have to be sown extra early in the year, say in January, there is more risk of this fungus appearing. Should it do so, at the very first signs water with Cheshunt Compound, which can be made as follows. Mix 2 parts of finely divided copper sulphate with 11 parts of *fresh* ammonium carbonate, also finely ground, by shaking in a bottle, and store the mixture for 24 hours in a tightly stoppered bottle. For use, dissolve 1 oz. in a little hot water and make up to 2 gallons with soft water. This should not be done in metal vessels, but a well-painted watering-can may be used.

WATERING. This is one of the most important operations at this stage in the life of the plant, and the full technique can really only be learned by practice. Principles to be observed are as follows. The water itself and the watering-can must be scrupulously clean. Use a watering-can with a very fine rose and mainly water in the morning so that any surplus moisture will have time to drain off before nightfall. The seedlings, being extremely fragile, must never be allowed to become really dry. This is one of the commonest causes of failure. A good method of ensuring thorough watering of very fine seeds, which are apt to be washed away by overhead watering, is by placing the container in a shallow dish of water and allowing it to soak until the moisture can be seen to reach the surface of the soil. This will ensure that there are no dry patches anywhere.

SHADING. Even half an hour's bright drying sunshine is sufficient to kill young seedlings. Only shade, however, when necessary and remove shading on every possible occasion, giving increasing air and light as the seedlings grow. On the other hand avoid excessive moisture.

PRICKING OUT. This is the expression given to the operation of transferring the tiny seedlings to another container, seed tray, or pan. As soon as the seedlings are large enough to handle, prick them out into trays, placing the young plants 2 or 3 in. apart each way, according to their size. The same principles again apply. Use a similar compost, only with a little less sand, and see that it is on no account sticky but working freely. Fill the boxes fairly firmly and absolutely evenly, there must be no hollow patches; water thoroughly, shade, and keep without much ventilation for a day or two until the seedlings begin to grow, afterwards giving increasing light and air. When pricking out the tiny seedlings lift them with extreme care in order not to damage the very fragile stem and roots which may be mortally injured by careless handling. A pointed stick is often useful for easing the soil underneath (Pl. 7a) and in the case of extremely small seedlings a stick with a tiny fork at the end of it (Pl. 7d) is a practical method of handling the little plant. A pointed stick or dibber is used to make a

29

convenient sized hole and the roots of the seedling are carefully inserted (Pl. 7b). The hole is then gently but firmly closed with the dibber so that the roots of the seedling are in intimate contact with the surrounding soil.

A very frequent error in this operation, and one which causes the loss of many seedlings among beginners, is that the neck only of the seedling is firmed, leaving the root in a hollow. The opposite should be ensured: see that the *roots* are properly firmed, the neck and the surrounding surface of the soil will be adequately firmed by subsequent waterings. The same principle applies when transplanting the seedling from the tray to the open ground. Firm the root and see that it is in intimate contact with the soil everywhere, the surface soil round the stem of the plant will always be adequately filled up and firmed by subsequent rains and working of the soil by hoeing, etc. When the seedlings are large enough to plant out, thoroughly harden them off before doing so. A good routine rule is to spray all boxes with a general insecticide before planting out.

7(*a*)

7. Pricking out young seedlings into boxes. (*a*) Removing young seed-lings of French marigolds with a pointed stick or label. (*b*) Pricking out into boxes. The roots of the seedlings are made firm by the dibber. (*c*) Watering the boxes of seedlings after pricking out. (*d*) Pricking out fine seedlings of begonia, the seedling is held with a forked stick.

7(b)

7(c)

(d)

8. Half-hardy
annuals planted
out after danger
of frost is
past. In the
foreground
are dianthus
seedlings.

PLANNING OF TIMES OF SOWING AND PLANTING OUT.
One very important point may be mentioned here and that is so
to arrange the times of sowing that each lot of seedlings is ready
for planting out just at the time it is safe to do so. There is no
more frequent cause of the failure of half-hardy annuals than to
have the seedling plants ready for planting out too soon, with the
result that they have to be kept in the boxes too long and thereby
become root-bound and suffer a check from which the plants
never recover. The same applies to the times of sowing outside.
The times of sowing are of vital importance and the only way one
can find out the optimum time for one's own garden is by keeping
careful records for each plant grown, and, by trial and error,
determining the very best time. A very great assistance, too, in the
busy time of spring and early summer is to arrange times of
sowing so that the times of pricking out or planting out are
spaced, so that one's limited time is used to the best advantage.

9. Biennials. Lining out seedling foxgloves in a nursery bed in late summer.

Biennials

These are sown in spring and early summer and come into full flower the following year. Good examples for garden conditions in England are Canterbury bell, sweet william, foxgloves, sweet rocket, and honesty. On the whole the principles of cultivation are very similar to those for annuals. The best time to sow is from April to May and June but, within reason, sow as early as practicable so that there is time for the plant to become fully grown before planting out in the autumn. A suitable part of the garden should be reserved for a seed bed for such plants, for example a sheltered position which can be shaded when required. The soil should be well cultivated, clean, and in good heart, and worked down to a fine tilth before sowing. Sow in shallow drills and prick out into nursery lines, say 12–15 in. apart with the plants 6–9 in. apart in the row, in showery weather as soon as the seedlings can be handled.

B

33

10. Hollyhock seedlings in a nursery bed.

11. Polyanthus seedlings in nursery beds showing method of shading.

2 · In the Garden

The Annual Border

Annual and biennial flowering plants, in a carefully arranged group by themselves, can make a picture of much beauty and by a suitable choice of subjects and carefully arranged times of sowing, a brilliant display can be obtained over a considerable period of time.

For the annual border proper, a position more or less by itself is probably best. The side of a path leading to the garage and skirting the part of the garden devoted to vegetables, would be a suitable site for such a border, other factors, such as soil and aspect, being satisfactory (Pl. 12). Another situation might be narrow borders on each side of a central path leading to the front door (Pl. 13), the beds being filled with bulbs in the spring, or annual borders might be used to flank a path leading from a

12. Nicotiana and other annuals bordering a small path of crazy paving.

13. Nemesias beside a path leading to a front door.

formal part of the garden to a small orchard. The south slope of a wide shallow ditch, dry of course in summer, can be made beautiful by this means and many other such positions will offer themselves in most gardens.

14. A fine double border of annuals at Great Missenden.

PRINCIPLES OF ARRANGEMENT. The main principle in the creation of such a border is informal arrangement, the subjects being grouped in irregular patches which tend to run into each other in a natural way rather like the patches of wild flowers one sees on the roadside and along the hedgerows in the country. In addition to the outlines of the groups being arranged irregularly, the heights of the plants should be grouped informally, with some of the taller plants occasionally brought fairly close up to the front; the whole effect will be natural-looking and completely informal in every respect (Pl. 14). With regard to colour arrangement, whether in blending colours or vivid contrasts, this is entirely a matter for individual taste. The material available is abundant. Here again, keeping a note-book and making careful notes when the border is in flower, is the best method of achieving the desired effect.

CONSTRUCTION AND SOWING. Points of cultivation already described must be strictly adhered to: early and deep cultivation, keeping the soil free from weeds, manuring, early staking, and so on. With regard to the method of sowing, if the soil is good and quite free from weeds, after the outlines of the patches have been marked out by sand, the seeds may be sown broadcast. On the other hand a simple practical method found useful in many gardens, after getting the border down to the required tilth for sowing, is to use the back of the rake to make drills at the required distance according to the height of the plants. (See Pls 15 *a–f*.)

15(*a*)

15(*b*)

15. Preparing and sowing the annual border. (*a*) Areas marked out after raking. (*b*) Making drills with a hoe. (*c*) Another method of making drills. (*d*) Sowing the seeds. (*e*) A convenient method of covering the seed and filling the drill.

15(c)

15(d)

15(e)

39

15(f). Shallow drills can also be filled in and the seed covered by a rake.

Another method sometimes used is to drill the border the whole length longitudinally in shallow drills 9 in. apart and mark the outline of the patches with sand. According to the size to which the plant will eventually grow at maturity, sow every drill or every other drill as required. Sowing in drills will allow for hoeing between the rows right up to the time the plants meet, and for getting about the border more easily for thinning, staking, etc.

When the plants are fully grown, the ground will be completely covered and no lines seen. A simple method for protecting the seed bed after sowing, is to cover the whole border lightly with twiggy stakes. These keep off cats and most small birds (Pl. 16).

The Mixed Border

In the mixed border, which may be a combination of flowering shrubs, herbaceous plants, lilies, and spring bulbs, room should also be found for annual and biennial flowering plants. Properly placed and selected with care, they will increase enormously the interest and colour of such a border. Here again the range of colours available, also the times of flowering, can be especially valuable (Pl. 17).

40

16. Protecting the border from birds and cats after the seed has been sown.

17. A fine example of a mixed border combining shrubs, herbaceous plants, and annuals.

Good examples of mixed borders can be seen in gardens up and down the country. It may be a wide border backed by a brick wall, on which are placed such perennial plants as climbing roses, clematis, honeysuckle, and also suitable annual climbing plants. In front of the wall shrubs may be planted at fairly wide intervals, both for flowering and foliage effect, their size being kept in proportion by skilful pruning. Suitable subjects would be Ceanothus 'Gloire de Versailles' and other varieties, *Chaenomeles lagenaria* (*Pyrus japonica*), *Acer negundo* and its varieties, *Osmanthus delavayi*, and other evergreens. The choice is a wide one, and a variety of possibilities can be found in any good book on shrubs. In between the shrubs many excellent positions will be found for lilies and other bulbous and herbaceous plants. Wide spaces should be left for the sowing of hardy annuals, using such subjects as larkspur, clumps of sweet pea, lavatera, nigella, Shirley poppy, and so on; also half-hardy annuals, such as the new types of hybrid sunflower, arctotis, petunia, verbena, and many others. These borders will give continuous colour and interest from early spring to late autumn.

The Greenhouse

Even in a garden devoted principally to hardy plants, a greenhouse heated sufficiently to keep out the frost, with the addition of a few cold frames, will add considerable interest. Besides raising plants from seed in the spring for planting out in the open later, the greenhouse can be invaluable for growing annuals and biennials to flower in pots. There are many suitable subjects, easily grown, and flowering nearly all the year round. Fuller details are given in Chapter 3.

Cut Flowers

Space should also be reserved in every garden for annuals and biennials grown entirely and solely for cut flowers for the house. It is better that the position should be somewhere by itself. When fully grown these plants can be cut right down to the ground, thus getting the full length of stem and avoiding cutting into the main flower border with the risk of spoiling its appearance (Pl. 18).

18. Part of a cutting border with everlastings (*Helipterum*) and antirrhinums.

The varieties available for cut flowers are numerous. Particularly useful for autumn sowing in the open are sweet peas, tall double godetias, Shirley poppies (both the double and single flowering forms), cornflowers, and larkspurs with their very wide range of colouring and extremely good lasting qualities. Many other subjects are suitable for this purpose. (See list on p. 249.)

Decorative Value for floral arrangements

Some unusual decorative effects can also be obtained from quite a number of annuals: these have been found of great value by the many floral societies up and down the country. Bells of Ireland (*Moluccella laevis*) (Pls 128 and 129), Snow on the Mountain (*Euphorbia marginata*), Orach (*Atriplex hortensis*), the pale green form of Love-lies-bleeding (*Amaranthus*), and so on. Wide use can be made of annuals and biennials grown especially for the indoor decoration of the home, whether for the flowers, fruits (Pl. 19), or foliage. Some of the everlasting flowers make charming vases of colour for winter decoration, such as *Helichrysum*, *Helipterum* (Pl. 18), and *Limonium* (Pl. 119). The flower heads should be cut when newly opened and still quite young, and hung in a light airy shed or room to dry. A full list of suitable varieties will be found on p. 249.

Some hints on cutting and subsequent treatment may be useful. The stems of annuals are very soft and often fragile, so have a good knife for cutting with a blade kept sharp. This is of great importance and cannot be emphasized too strongly. If one cannot use a knife, *sharp* secateurs or *sharp* scissors are the next best.

In cutting, always pick fresh young newly opened flowers. This makes all the difference to their lasting. In the Composites, the

19. A decorative arrangement made from the seed heads of annual grasses.

daisy family, watch the centre disc and pick when the outer ring of stamens only is showing. If the whole centre is showing the stamens and is yellow, this means the flower head has been open for some time and will soon be past its best.

Try to pick the flowers on a quiet day, in the evening or early morning, never let them lie in the hot sun, and put them into water as quickly as possible. Place them in deep, wide containers in water at air temperature in a cool, airy, and shaded place, with a north light. Plunge the flowers in water right up to their necks and leave for some hours. Should the flowers be travelling by post or hand, leave them to soak for 12 hours.

Remember that flowers and stems are living material, and that the cells of which they are composed are exceedingly delicate and quickly die when exposed to the air. The ideal method of picking would be to cut the stem actually under water so that the cut surface is never exposed to the air, but where this cannot be done leave the cut end of the stem exposed to the air for as short a time as possible. For the flower to keep alive, the water must be drawn up through the living cells and if they have been killed by being exposed to the wind and air too long, they cannot absorb water.

Plants vary much in their response to cutting. The stems of some, such as the varieties of tall double godetias, will subsequently open their flower buds right to the tip, especially if the leaves are removed.

A useful tip for reviving cut flowers which have become wilted is to place them immediately into very hot water, as hot as can be borne by the hand. This can accomplish wonders in reviving withered flowers.

Compositions can also be made with whole plants lifted from the open ground or grown in pots of various sizes for the purpose. Many annuals and biennials lend themselves to this use. Empty fireplaces can be adorned, and flat containers can be made into miniature gardens which give pleasure for weeks. By trial and error it can be discovered which plants lift best in this way. All bulbous subjects usually lift well in full flower. A foxglove plant can be lifted in full flower, placed in a container, and never 'turn a hair'. So can *Penstemon glaber*, whose hybrids with their lovely pastel shades of pink and blue blend so admirably.

45

When it is desired to lift a whole plant with its roots from the open ground, do so either very early in the morning or late evening. Use a sharp worn spade for preference, take a good 'ball' to hold the main body of roots, have a convenient-sized piece of light sacking or hessian at hand and tie up the ball of roots immediately the plant is lifted. Put in a cool shaded place and water thoroughly both the root and overhead. Many subjects will lift quite easily in full flower in this way, especially biennials. Some of the annuals are more difficult and these should be sown in pots which have been plunged in the open ground and can be lifted intact as required.

Annuals in the Rock Garden

In spite of the objections of certain purists, most gardeners will agree today that many annual and biennial flowering plants can be of great value in the rock garden. *Anagallis, Limnanthes,*

20. Antirrhinum 'Little Gem' making summer colour in the rock garden.

46

Ionopsidium, Leptosiphon (*Gilia*), the dwarf forms of *Echium plantagineum*, and many others will look very much at home there, and make bright patches during the summer and early autumn months. (See list on p. 248.)

Climbers

The many forms of climbing annuals can be used with beautiful effect in the flower garden. What is more beautiful than a vigorous hedge of sweet peas or nasturtiums climbing through a hedge, a fence covered by canary creeper, an arbour clothed by *Cobaea scandens* or the curious and interesting ornamental gourds? (See list on p. 248.)

Sunny Banks

Many climbing annuals and the more dwarf-growing plants are particularly useful for covering rough banks, filling odd corners and dry sunny places. Many can be sown where they are to flower, but in some cases it leads to more certain results if the seedlings are given a start by being sown in a cold frame in little pots and, when established, planted out into their flowering positions. Taking this small extra trouble may make all the difference between success and failure, if the terrain is somewhat difficult. (See list on pp. 247 and 248.)

Sweet-scented Plants

Annuals are particularly rich in plants with fragrant flowers. Full use should be made of these and positions carefully chosen for using them, placing them in corners near seats and sunny sheltered spots where the full value of the scents can be enjoyed. Mignonette, with its clean delicious fragrance, is not used nearly enough in gardens nowadays. Other sweet-smelling plants are night-scented stock, verbena, stocks (Pl. 21), sweet rocket, tobacco, evening primrose, and also the Californian *Oenothera trichocalyx* with a scent like honeysuckle. (See p. 250.)

Further examples of the uses of annuals in gardens may be mentioned. A planting of tobacco plant, *Nicotiana alata* (Pl. 12),

47

21. Sweet-scented stocks in a fine double border.

in light shade, say under tall trees where the branches are kept high, can be very effective. The light shade ensures that the flowers will remain open during the day. As long as the plants are assured of sufficient water and the soil well prepared, they will flower the whole summer in such a position. *Collinsia bicolor*, that attractive low growing hardy annual, besides being useful in the mixed border, is beautiful sown in drifts in light woodland or the wild garden.

Plants for brick paths and pavings

Virginian stock, *Limnanthes douglasii*, and *Platystemon californicus* and other such plants are very suitable for sowing broadcast on an old brick paved path or courtyard – and virginian stock, particularly, will do perfectly well in a north light without direct sunshine. Mignonette very often succeeds admirably if sown in patches actually on the edges of a path. *Lavatera trimestris*

Splendens makes a beautiful flowering hedge, sown thinly along the side of a path skirting a paddock or orchard. It can be sown in place with the minimum of trouble and will flower the whole summer, besides providing abundant flower stems for cutting.

Colour

Colour schemes, whether matching tones or contrasting colours, are very interesting to work out with annuals and biennials. The 'Giant Primrose' foxglove contrasts most effectively with *Delphinium belladonna* 'Pale Blue' especially as they flower at exactly the same time. The rose-pink and deep violet-blue varieties of the annual *Salvia horminum* make a charming combination. The cool pastel shades of *Penstemon glaber* hybrids make an harmonious mixture of rose-pink, bright blue, purple, and white. Similar cool tones can also be found in *Verbascum phoeniceum*, which succeeds in semi-shade. Rose-pink and mauve-purple shades of linaria, the rich range of colouring to be found in a mixed bed of viscaria and nemesia are satisfying mixtures of colour for use in many parts of the garden. A mixture of dimorphotheca varieties in tones of orange, salmon, flame, and ivory is very effective in an open sunny situation.

Annuals in mixtures of this kind can find a most useful place in our gardens but one word of warning must be added. When pricking out mixtures from a seed bed or pan, take care to prick out the tiny seedlings just as they come. Never select only the largest and strongest. Many of the finer colours can be lost in this way.

In discussing the uses of annuals and biennials in the flower garden, chance appearances of self-sown plants in parts of the garden have given much pleasure by their happy appropriateness and charming aspect; for example, seen on a sunny November day, a chance grouping of a few irregularly placed honesty plants with their silvery empty seed heads shining against dark green foliage. Chance plants of tall sweet rocket, alongside a path in an open woodland glade, or a group of the modern coloured foxgloves, especially the pure white, make a delightful picture (Pl. 22).

49

22. Foxgloves in an open woodland at The R.H.S. Gardens, Wisley.

Again, in the rock garden the association of, say, *Platystemon californicus* (Cream-cups of California) with the blue *Nemophila menziesii* is particularly happy. Such examples could be multiplied but these illustrations may demonstrate a further sense of fascination in the growing of these plants. It is also sometimes possible to repeat such successful chance arrangements.

3 · In the Cool Greenhouse

Even in a garden devoted mainly to outdoor plants, a glass-house together with a few cold frames will be found to be of the greatest possible use. If sufficient heat is available to keep out frost, better and more certain results can be obtained with the wide and useful range of half-hardy annuals, and even in the raising from seed of some hardy annuals and biennials. Although, by the use of cold frames only, quite good results can be obtained with skill and careful attention, control is much easier and good results more easily obtained in a cool greenhouse which has just sufficient heat to exclude frost. The little seedlings are more easily examined and handled. The air temperature and moisture content can be more simply controlled. A few cold frames to which seedlings in boxes or pans can be transferred as soon as conditions allow, can treble the capacity of such a house.

Besides raising flowering plants for the garden it is possible to grow a large number of annuals and biennials for flowering in pots during the greater part of the year, provided suitable subjects are chosen. These will be found very useful too for bringing into the dwelling house and for using as cut flowers. Instructions for sowing seeds under glass and pricking out seedlings have already been given.

Certain annuals which do not transplant easily, such as linaria, viscaria, and eschscholzia, may be sown thinly directly in the pots where they are to flower. When the seedlings are large enough to handle they should be thinned down to, say, three, four, or five plants according to the size of pot. Most annuals, however, can be pricked out with success if the operation is carried out carefully and the seedlings kept close and shaded for a few days until the tiny plant begins to grow again. Pricking out should always be done when the seedlings are quite tiny. The compost for growing annuals in pots should always be on the light side, with enough sharp sand and well-decayed leaf mould to make it porous. Thorough drainage is essential, and the pots must be well scrubbed before using to make sure they are

51

23. Annuals and foliage plants in a cool greenhouse.

perfectly clean. Compost and pots should be sterilized before
using. The main general essentials for growing conditions are
light and air with just enough heat in winter to keep out frost and
maintain buoyancy in the atmosphere.

Where the main purpose of the greenhouse is to raise half-
hardy plants for planting out in the garden and to grow flowering
plants in pots, for cut flowers and for bringing into the dwelling
house, the main display of bloom will be during spring and summer. It is quite possible, however, with a little management, and
the addition of cold frames, to have some plants in flower
throughout the year. A full list of annuals and biennials suitable
for growing in such a greenhouse will be found at the end of this
chapter. In the meantime it may be helpful to give an example of
the kind of succession which might be obtained, starting with
Christmas-time and the dead of winter, which is the most difficult
time of all for such plants.

24. Petunias and lobelias in a cool greenhouse.

That delightful winter flowering plant the Persian cyclamen can be treated as a biennial and from seed sown in August–October one can have it in full flower in 15–16 months, i.e. for the following Christmas twelve months. Sow the seed singly half an inch deep and two inches apart in pans in a compost consisting of half loam and half leaf soil or peat, with enough sand to ensure good drainage. Place the August sowings in cold frames on a cool ash bottom and keep moist and shaded so that they are cool. On germination, which is apt to be somewhat erratic, remove shading and admit air but protect from direct sunlight and keep cool. Remove the seedlings to the greenhouse at the end of September and keep moist and shaded from hot sun. When they have developed 3 or 4 leaves pot singly into 3-in. pots and finally into 5- or 6-in. pots by June for flowering. The seedlings may be transferred to cold frames once more during the summer, and brought into the greenhouse in the autumn for flowering. At no stage should the young plants be allowed to become pot-bound. For final potting use a compost of two parts loam, one part leaf soil or peat, one part well-decayed manure, with enough sharp sand to ensure good drainage. To this compost add 1 oz. superphosphate, and 2 oz. of hoof and horn meal per bushel. Lime in any form must not be added. Cyclamen revel in moisture during all stages of growth, appreciate a humid atmosphere, and delight in sprayings of clean water several times daily until the approach of the flowering period. As the autumn approaches give air freely on good days to ensure a buoyant atmosphere, reducing the waterings; as winter approaches damping down is unnecessary. At this season a night temperature of 55 to 60 degrees with a little ventilation is advisable. The plants will remain in bloom for three months on end.

'Beauty of Nice' stocks may also be brought into flower during the winter months, details for which are given later. *Felicia* (*Agathaea*) *pappei*, a charming blue daisy from South Africa, if sown in May or June and potted on as required, will flower during January and February. Nemesias and Gleam nasturtiums will also flower in pots at Christmas-time if sown in July–August and if enough light can be provided.

Another most useful plant for flowering during winter and early spring in the cool greenhouse is *Primula malacoides*, that free flowering dainty primula discovered by Forrest in China in 1908. The range of colour and habit has been so much increased that this is now one of our most useful greenhouse flowering plants. Again the secret of cultivation is to maintain cool moist conditions in the early stages and to use a light, well-drained compost. Sow in June–July for flowering in February–March. The flowers are also very useful for table decoration, and sprays of blooms of mixed colours are attractive when worn on a dress. The colours now include clear lavender, mauve, purple, pale pink, deep pink, and crimson, in addition to the original lavender-mauve. These may be followed by that decorative plant from the Canary Islands – the cineraria, full particulars of which are given under that heading. (See p. 172.)

In April and May the South American annual *Schizanthus pinnatus* will come into flower (Pl. 25). In addition to the usual

25. *Schizanthus* and cineraria in a cool greenhouse.

sowings in August and September, a sowing of this useful plant
may be made in spring to produce plants to flower in 5-in. pots
in August. These will produce long stems suitable for cutting for
vases and general table decoration, proving a most useful
addition to the cut flowers available at that time.

From May onwards during the summer the choice of annuals
and biennials to flower in pots in the cool greenhouse is very
wide. Many annuals may be sown in September and October to
flower under such conditions during April and May. Nemesia,
ursinia (Pl. 26b), lobelia (sow in August), dimorphotheca, salpiglossis, clarkia, and annual chrysanthemum, are all easily grown
and have bright, vivid flowers.

For late summer and autumn, Swan River Daisy in 5-in. pots
makes an unusual decorative plant. Other suitable plants include
Hunnemannia, celosia (both the plume and crested forms),

26. Four good plants for a cool greenhouse. Each is a single plant. (*a*) *Celosia cristata*. (*b*) *Ursinia anethoides*. (*c*) Swan River Daisy (*Brachycome iberidifolia*). (*d*) A young jacaranda a few months old grown from seed for foliage effect.

dahlias – both the Dwarf Coltness and Dwarf Border sections from seed sown in April, *Exacum affine* whose scent fills a room, the chimney campanula (*Campanula pyramidalis*), the Chinese delphinium, nemesias from a June–July sowing, 'East Lothian' stocks, and *Celsia arcturus* from a sowing made in March and flowered in 5-in. pots.

These are only a few of the flowering plants easily raised from seed which may be used for the decoration of the cool greenhouse.

26(b)

26(c)

26(d)

Annuals and Biennials including a few short-lived Perennials for growing in pots in the Cool Greenhouse

NAME	TIME TO SOW	DUE TO FLOWER	APPROX. LENGTH OF FLOWERING PERIOD	HEIGHT
Acroclinium, *see under* **Helipterum**				
Ageratum	Jan–Feb	May–June	10–12 weeks	1–2 ft
Alonsoa	Jan–Feb	April–May	8–10 weeks	12–15 in.
Anchusa	Jan–Feb	April–May	8–10 weeks	18 in.
Antirrhinum	Aug–Sept	May	8–10 weeks	12 in. to 3 ft
	Jan–Feb	June (end)	8–10 weeks	(according to variety)
Arctotis	February	May	12 weeks	18–30 in.
Begonia (fibrous-rooted)	Feb–March	August	12 weeks	12 in.
Begonia (tuberous-rooted)	February	August	12 weeks	12 in.
Browallia speciosa major	March	September	12 weeks	2 ft
Calceolaria	May–June	April–May	6 weeks	18–30 in.
Calendula	February	May	8–10 weeks	12–18 in.
	and at intervals to flower more or less throughout the year			
Campanula medium (Canterbury bell)	May–June	May (12 months)	6 weeks	2–2½ ft
Campanula isophylla (Basket Campanula)	March–April	June (12 months)	10–12 weeks	trailing
Campanula pyramidalis (Chimney Campanula)	March–April	August (12 months)	10–12 weeks	4–5 ft
Celsia arcturus	March–April	June	10–12 weeks	18 in. to 2 ft
Celsia cretica	March	July	8–10 weeks	5–6 ft
Celosia	August	January onwards	8–10 weeks	5–6 ft
Chrysanthemum, Annual	Feb–March	July–Oct	10–12 weeks	1–2 ft
Chrysanthemum, Perennial –	Feb–March	June	6 weeks	18 in.
Cascade and Charm	Feb–March	October (end)	8–10 weeks	5–7 ft as Cascade
				18 in. to 2 ft as Charm

58

	April–June	Jan–April (according to time of sowing and treatment)	6 weeks	15 in. to 3 ft (according to variety)
Cineraria			6 weeks	
Clarkia	September	May	6 weeks	3–4 ft
	Feb–March	June	8–10 weeks	2 ft
Cornflower	October	March–April	6–8 weeks	3–4 ft
	Feb–March	May–June	6–8 weeks	3–4 ft
Cyclamen, Persian	Aug–Oct	November (12 months)	12 weeks	12–15 in.
Datura	March	August	8–10 weeks	2–3 ft
Delphinium grandiflorum	July–August	June	8–10 weeks	15–18 in.
	Feb–March	July	8–10 weeks	15–18 in.
Dianthus chinensis Heddewigii	Feb–March	June	6 weeks	12 in.
	September	May	6–8 weeks	12 in.
Dimorphotheca aurantiaca and varieties	January	May	10–12 weeks	12–15 in.
Dimorphotheca chrysanthemifolia	July	April	10–12 weeks	18 in. to 2 ft
	March	July	10–12 weeks	18 in. to 2 ft
Exacum affine	March	August	10–12 weeks	15 in.
Felicia pappei	May–June	Jan–Feb	10–12 weeks	15–18 in.
Francoa ramosa	May–June	July (12 months)	6–8 weeks	2–3 ft
Gilia coronopifolia	September	July (12 months)	8–10 weeks	3–4 ft
Helipterum including Acroclinium and Rhodanthe	February	May (end)	6–8 weeks	12–15 in.
	Sept–Oct	April–May	6–8 weeks	12–15 in.
Hunnemannia	March	July–Sept	10–12 weeks	15–18 in.
	August	May onwards	12–14 weeks	15–18 in.
Impatiens balsamina	March	July–Aug	6–8 weeks	12–18 in.
Impatiens holstii and sultani	March	August	10–12 weeks	9–15 in.
Kochia	March–April	Foliage plant	Colours in autumn	3 ft

59

Annuals and Biennials including a few short-lived Perennials for growing in pots in the Cool Greenhouse

NAME	TIME TO SOW	DUE TO FLOWER	APPROX. LENGTH OF FLOWERING PERIOD	HEIGHT
Larkspur	February	June (end)	6–8 weeks	2–3 ft
	September	May	8–10 weeks	4–5 ft
Limonium (Statice) sinuatum and suworowii	February	July	8–10 weeks	18 in.
Lobelia erinus and	February	June	10–12 weeks	6 in.
Lobelia ramosa	July	April–May	10–12 weeks	6 in.
Matthiola, *see under* Stocks				
Mignonette	Jan–March	June	10–12 weeks	12 in.
	June	Autumn and winter	10–12 weeks	12 in.
	Aug–Sept	Spring	10–12 weeks	12 in.
Mimulus	February	July–August	8–10 weeks	12–15 in.
Myosotis (Forget-me-not)	June–July	November onwards	8–10 weeks	12 in.
Nasturtium (Tropaeolum)	Feb–March	May (middle)	8–10 weeks	15 in. to 5 ft
	July	October	8–10 weeks	15 in. to 5 ft
	October	Early spring	8–10 weeks	15 in. to 5 ft
Nemesia	January	May	8–10 weeks	12–15 in.
	March	June–July	8–10 weeks	12–15 in.
	June–July	Sept–Oct	8–10 weeks	12–15 in.
	July–Aug	Nov–Dec	8–10 weeks	12–15 in.
Nicotiana	Feb–March	May (end)	10–12 weeks	18–30 in.
	September	April–May	10–12 weeks	2–4 ft
Petunia	February	June	12–14 weeks	12–18 in.
Phlox drummondii	February	June	12–14 weeks	12–18 in.
	September	May	12–14 weeks	12–18 in.
Primula malacoides	June–July	January	3 months	12–15 in.
Primula obconica	January (end)	October (end)	5 months	12 in.
Primula sinensis	March–June	Dec–Jan	8–10 weeks	12–18 in.

Rehmannia	August (end)	May	8–10 weeks	4–5 ft
Rhodanthe, *see under* Helipterum				
Salpiglossis	Jan–Feb	June	6–8 weeks	2–3 ft
	September	April–May	6–8 weeks	3–4 ft
Schizanthus	Aug–Sept	April–May	8–10 weeks	18–30 in.
	February	August	4–6 weeks	18 in. to 2 ft
Stocks (Matthiola)				
10-week (Gt Perfection)	March–April	July–August	6–8 weeks	15–18 in.
Intermediate vars (E. Lothian)	March	Aug–Sept	8–10 weeks	15–18 in.
Winter-flowering vars				
(Beauty of Nice)	June–August	Dec–Feb	8–10 weeks	18 in. to 2 ft
Brompton (spring flowering)	July–August	April–May	6–8 weeks	18 in. to 2 ft
Swan River Daisy (Brachycome)	Feb–March	May–June	10–12 weeks	12–15 in.
Sweet Sultan	Sept–Oct	May	10–12 weeks	18–24 in.
	Feb–March	June–July	10–12 weeks	18–24 in.
Torenia	Feb–March	July	8–10 weeks	12–15 in.
Trachelium	Feb–March	July	10 weeks	18 in. to 2 ft
	July–Aug	June	10 weeks	18 in. to 2 ft
Trachymene (Didiscus)	February	July	8–10 weeks	12–18 in.
	Aug–Sept	May–June	8–10 weeks	12–18 in.
Tropaeolum, *see under* Nasturtium				
Ursinia	Feb–March	May	8–10 weeks	12–15 in.
Viscaria	October	April–May	6–8 weeks	12–15 in.
	March	June–July	6–8 weeks	12–15 in.
Wallflower (especially early-flowering varieties)				
Zinnia	June	December onwards	8–10 weeks	18 in. to 2 ft
	Feb–March	July	6–8 weeks	2–2½ ft
	June–July	September	6–8 weeks	2–2½ ft

The above list could be considerably extended if space had allowed. The reader is recommended to try many other annual and biennial plants for decorating the cool greenhouse. Successional sowings can also be further extended.

4 · How new garden varieties have arisen

In the development of interest in gardening, man noticed the flowering plants which he found growing in the countryside around him and began to introduce the most decorative of them into his garden. Among these were a number of annual and biennial species. The corn marigold and the familiar blue cornflower are examples of annual flowering wild plants which have been brought from the field into our gardens.

As the world was explored and more and more countries visited by people interested in flowering plants, seeds of hundreds of species were brought back to this country and the resulting plants introduced into our gardens. Thus have arisen many of our most decorative annuals and biennials today.

When these plants were brought into cultivation and, therefore, under close observation, it was noticed that in many of them variations occurred. These appeared either in the habit of the plant, such as taller, dwarfer, or more vigorous individuals than the type; or in the time of flowering, the size and colouring of the flowers, and so on. In gardens, this kind of variability was particularly apparent in the case of annual and biennial flowering plants since they have to be raised annually from seed.

Now the seed is that part of the plant which has arisen from the flower, and is the result of the development of a fertilized egg cell arising from the union of two sexual cells or gametes; the male gamete is contained in the pollen grain and the female gamete in the ovule produced in the ovary found in the centre of the flower. Each seed, therefore, is a completely new individual with all the exciting possibilities which that involves. There may thus arise considerable differences from either of the parents. This is the fundamental fact which has given rise to nearly all new garden forms. Further, the fact that annuals and biennials are raised from seed year by year, means that the chance of new forms appearing in such plants must be very much greater than in horticultural varieties of vegetatively propagated plants such as herbaceous perennials, flowering shrubs, and so on. This is well proved by horticultural experience. In the title of this chapter, the term 'arisen' is used deliberately with regard to these new varieties.

These new forms or variations arise spontaneously through the variability inherent in living things.

In a hybrid or cross between two varieties or species of plants a recombination of characters occurs. These are presented to the gardener by chance and his selection of the desirable garden form depends upon his ability and skill to spot and select these variations as they occur. It will thus be seen that one essential condition in the introduction of such new desirable forms into our gardens is the man with the 'seeing eye', the gardener who has an 'eye for a plant'. He must first know his plants intimately and secondly he must know what he wants, and thus be able to select and choose the new forms presented to him. In other words, this faculty of the 'seeing eye', the recognizing of the good garden plant *when he sees it*, is one of the essential qualities of the successful plant breeder.

New forms in garden plants raised from seed thus arise after chance or deliberate hybridization. But they may also arise as chance sports or mutations, changes within the plant itself. Sometimes the change is fairly obvious such as the first wavy petalled or Spencer sweet pea. This mutation arose simultaneously in one or two gardens in this country. Although the variation appears in this case fairly easy to see, it may be that this form had occurred before in gardens but the 'seeing eye' was absent. No one had noticed it.

Many other examples of such mutations or sports could be given. Thus have arisen the dwarf or Cupid sweet pea, which forms a dense mat on the ground and does not climb. The orange-coloured varieties in godetia, the first of which was 'Sybil Sherwood', originated from one plant which appeared in a large bed of mixed colours. This was noticed and selected by a keen gardener.

Fortunately for the gardener, these sports usually breed true straight away and a new strain can then be raised simply by isolating carefully from all other varieties. The dwarf cornflower known as 'Jubilee Gem', the first of the Carnation-Flowered type of African marigold, 'Guinea Gold', the dwarf Charm group of *Chrysanthemum indicum*, all arose in the same way, as chance mutations, selected by gardeners, and bred true to their respective characteristics.

A vast amount of work has been done over recent years by our scientists in research into the factors which govern inheritance in our flowering plants. Especially since the rediscovery of the description of the experiments carried out by Gregor Mendel, the Austrian monk, very much more is now known as to how and why these variations occur in plants. By this knowledge the skilled plant breeder can plan such changes and predict the results fairly accurately.

Another source of new garden forms is the deliberate crossing of two distinct varieties or species. For example, the new colours in the tall double forms of godetia were derived from a cross between *G. grandiflora*, the compact dwarf growing species, and *G. amoena*, the taller and looser-growing species (Pl. 27). Various shades of pink and red were found in *G. grandiflora* which were not found in the tall growing *G. amoena*, but by crossing the two species these colours in *G. grandiflora* were eventually transferred to a tall plant like *G. amoena*.

In the case mentioned above of Spencer sweet peas the form of the original wavy petalled mutation was quickly transferred, by crossing, to all the other known varieties. The same occurred with the double mutation in the garden nasturtium, known as 'Golden Gleam'. Golden yellow was the colour of the original mutation found in Mexico and, after introduction, this double form was transferred to all the known colours by crossing between the single forms in existence and the new double-flowered mutation.

Another source of new forms in plants is the chance doubling of the chromosomes. Chromosomes are thread-like structures forming the nucleus of all active cells including, of course, the germ cells in plants and animals. Chromosomes carry the bodies known as genes which are responsible for the whole hereditary character of the individual. They are the very essence of heredity. When sexual cells are produced, the number of chromosomes is exactly halved so that upon the union of the male and female

27. Godetia showing the tall bushy hybrid (centre) derived from the cross between *G. amoena* ♀, the tall plant on the left, and *G. grandiflora* ♂, the dwarf compact plant on the right.

gametes the resulting fertilized egg-cell contains once more the normal number of chromosomes for that species, half from the mother and half from the father. It sometimes happens, however, that for various reasons this reduction process does not take place and that, therefore, a doubling of the chromosomes arises, resulting

c

in the creation of a new individual. This may be the start of a new race or even of a new species. This doubling of the chromosomes is often shown in the production of larger plants of a giant form, with much larger flowers, more varied and with brighter colours and so on. Many new horticultural varieties have arisen in this way and have been selected by gardeners, without an understanding of their origin. The recent large-flowered forms of *Primula malacoides* with their wider range of colouring have arisen in this way (Pls 28 and 29). So have the modern forms of the garden daffodil, and the garden iris.

In the garden and in nature too, chance hybridization occurs both between different species and between forms within the species, thus giving birth to many new garden forms. The pink-flowered delphinium, first known as *D. ruysii* 'Pink Sensation', arose through a chance hybridization in the nursery of Messrs Ruys in Holland, between the dwarf growing, red-flowered *D. nudicaule* and the tall growing, blue-flowered *D. elatum*. This cross had been attempted artificially thousands of times before. How did it happen that a bumble bee managed to perform what

28. *Primula malacoides.* The original wild form, a photograph taken in Yunnan by George Forrest, who introduced this plant to cultivation.

29. A modern horti-
cultural variety of
Primula malacoides
showing the great
increase in size of
flower obtained by
breeding.

had hitherto proved impossible to man? What occurred was
probably this. The two species *D. elatum* and *D. nudicaule* were
growing side by side. Seed was collected from *D. nudicaule* which
usually breeds perfectly true. In this case, however, one plant
arose which appeared to be quite different from the type, being
much taller, with larger foliage, and when it flowered gave
purplish-coloured flowers. This was seeded in turn and from the
resulting seedlings was segregated the pink-flowered variety, now
known as 'Pink Sensation'.

The cytology of the two parent species gives the clue to the
origin of his new form. *D. nudicaule* is a diploid with sixteen
chromosomes and *D. elatum* is a tetraploid with thirty-two
chromosomes. The term 'diploid' refers to the number of
chromosomes. The number is constant within every species of
plant or animal. When a plant is referred to as 'diploid', it means
that it contains in its vegetative cells the normal number of
chromosomes for that species ($2x$) which is double the basic
number (x) found in the germ cells, i.e. the pollen or egg cells. A
tetraploid plant has four times the basic number ($4x$). It was

found that the new 'Pink Sensation' is a tetraploid with thirty-two chromosomes. What must have happened was that an unreduced *D. nudicaule* ($2x = 16$) egg cell was fertilized with a normal *D. elatum* pollen grain ($4x = 32$), having thus 16 chromosomes in its pollen grain, thus giving a fertile hybrid ($4x = 32$)

$$
\begin{array}{c|c}
\textit{D. nudicaule} \quad \times & \textit{D. elatum} \\
2x = 16 & 4x = 32 \\
\text{(unreduced egg)} & \text{(reduced pollen)} \\
\end{array}
$$
'Pink Sensation'
$$4x = 32$$

This chance upsetting of the normal chromosome reduction in a germ cell quite often happens in nature. What was so extraordinary in this case was the fact that a pollen grain of the other species happened to be carried by a bee to this flower, a lucky chance.

Man, however, has not been content to rest here; with his new knowledge of the processes of cell formation and reproduction, in his researches into the reproductive processes governing all life and its multitudinous variations, he has now learnt to induce sports or mutations in plants and thus produce the starting point of distinct new horticultural varieties. Professor Bauer of Berlin showed that by the action of X-rays the incidence of mutation in antirrhinums could be multiplied ten times, and these mutations bred true from seed.

It has been found that the action of the drug colchicine, when applied to young growing tissues in the active growing stage, has an influence in preventing the normal reduction of chromosomes in the early stages of cell division, thus inducing a doubling of the chromosomes and the creation of an entirely new plant with quite new breeding possibilities. Besides actually thus creating a new plant, a possibility of intercrossing two races or species, which was hitherto impossible, is created. Outstanding new garden varieties have already been made in this way. A good example is the marigold, Burpee's Red and Gold Hybrids. This has arisen from a fertile cross between the African and French marigolds, now made possible by the doubling of chromosomes induced by the action of the drug colchicine.

It is thus seen that science has assisted the trained plant breeder and seedsman to create new garden varieties. In addition it has shown him new ways of ensuring the trueness to type of his stocks of seeds. This is of the utmost importance to the practical gardener. It has been noticed that the first generation from an original cross usually results in plants quite even in growth and completely true to certain characteristics.

When it is desired to intercross two varieties and thus produce an even-growing 'first' family, the problem of emasculation or removal of the anthers of one of the parents before they shed their pollen, arises. In the case of a plant with fairly large flowers, say petunia, the seed bearing variety can be fairly easily 'emasculated' by carefully removing the stamens with the aid of forceps before they ripen, thus ensuring the cross when the pollen of the other variety is applied to the stigmas of the emasculated flowers. This is, of course, a fairly lengthy and expensive operation and is only possible when the results are so useful as to make the extra cost worthwhile. By careful observation and study, however, male sterile forms have been discovered in quite a number of garden plants. By producing strains breeding true to this characteristic, it is comparatively easy to produce a first generation family in quantity by growing rows of the male sterile form interspersed with the pollen bearing form. An F_1 or 'first filial' generation can thus now be produced in quantity and at a reasonable cost. This method of ensuring even growing stocks of garden varieties is becoming more and more used in commercial seed growing. The field of finding, selecting, and even inducing the production of new garden varieties is becoming wider.

There are, however, many still unsolved problems in this exciting pursuit and even many openings in which the interested and knowledgeable amateur gardener can take part. The study of plants and their garden forms is unending.

5 · How the gardener gets his seeds

It is, of course, the responsibility of the seedsman to provide seeds for the garden. Seedsmen either collect seeds in the wild for distribution or grow them as a crop to sell. This activity is now world wide. This is not the place to trace the history of seed growing in this country but a few facts on how seeds find their way into our gardens unfailingly year in and year out, may be of interest.

Quite a number of the seeds of the hardier plants are grown in this country, mainly in the south and east where the summer is drier and the sun warmer. The great bulk of the seed used in our gardens today comes, however, from countries with a climate warmer and more dependable for the thorough ripening and harvesting of seeds, such as France and Italy, Germany and Holland. Large quantities are also now grown in the U.S.A., mainly in California. The total crop grown and distributed of, say, one popular plant such as antirrhinum in California alone runs into many tons a year and when it is remembered that one ounce of antirrhinum seeds contains approximately two hundred thousand seeds, the scope of the undertaking can be appreciated. Antirrhinum is only one out of hundreds of other plants whose seeds are required annually in gardens today.

Moreover the actual growing and producing of seeds is only one branch of this great undertaking. Every one of the thousands of horticultural varieties of garden plants which have been produced with such skill and labour must be kept true and up to standard by careful isolation from like varieties to prevent contamination by bees, wind, and other pollinating agents. In addition stock or mother seed has to be selected each year to preserve the standard of the variety whether for colour of flower, habit of plant, earliness, or other characteristics.

In the matter of cultivation for seed, many and varied are the methods required. It may be fairly easy to grow a plant so that it comes to perfection of flowering, but to grow it on to produce a good crop of seed is often quite another thing, and frequently requires skilful cultivation and management. There are also the various techniques of harvesting, storage, and cleaning, which are being improved year by year. It is often an exciting race to get all crops harvested, cleaned, and delivered to the distributing centre in time for the spring demand. It is a tribute to the seed growers and seedsmen of this and other lands that our gardens are so seldom let down and that the seed we need is usually available when we want it.

New techniques are continually being evolved to aid seed growers. These often arise directly from investigations in pure science in our research stations. One recent example may be given. The new chrysanthemum group known as Charm does not flower normally until early November. This variety is grown from seeds sown in the early spring and comes into flower the same year, and therefore a crop of seeds is required annually. Now November is not a good month for setting and harvesting a crop of seed. However, by recent scientific research it has been

30. Thrashing of small parcels of stock or mother seeds by hand flail.

71

31. An old-fashioned method of thrashing broad beans with horse and roller.

found that the time of flowering of the chrysanthemum is strictly dependent upon the length of daylight, and flower buds are not formed until the days become shorter. Therefore by placing the plants being grown for seed in darkness for part of the day, they can be made to come into full flower in August instead of November. Thus a good set of seed can be ensured without upsetting the normal time of flowering of the plants grown from such seed. This is a good example of the use of pure research in up-to-date commercial practice.

Many ingenious methods are used for thrashing and cleaning the seeds of the varied horticultural seed crops. The machines used range from the largest and most elaborate of combine thrashers and harvesters down to small power-driven single-drum machines which simply knock out the seeds from the pods. It is interesting to note that the old-fashioned hand flail is still used, mainly for the purpose of thrashing small quantities of valuable stock or mother seeds (Pl. 30).

Having thrashed the seeds from the pods many methods are used to get the seeds down to a good growing sample fit for sowing in the garden. The machines used employ the principle of gravity (simply blowing out the chaff and light seed and leaving the good), also centrifugal force, magnets, and various electrical devices. In spite of the number of clever mechanical devices, some

72

32. Thrashing broccoli seeds by a small power-driven machine.

samples of seed still have to be finished off by picking over by hand, for example peas which have been discoloured by bad weather in harvesting. An ingenious method of removing peas holed by weevils is by passing the crop through a revolving inclined drum, inside which are inserted sharp needles pointing inwards. As the peas pass down the revolving drum all the peas with holes in them eventually get caught up by the sharp-pointed needles and so removed; thereby saving what used to be a considerable hand labour (Pl. 33).

In other machines seeds are made to pass over a smooth inclined plane down which the sound round seeds pass easily, whereas impurities and misshapen seeds stick and are so removed. Cloths of different textures are also used on such inclined planes for a similar purpose. Many, too, are the sizes and types of sieves used. In fact much ingenuity and great skill is shown in the methods used by seedsmen to ensure that gardeners receive a good, clean, viable sample of seed for sowing in their gardens.

33. A revolving drum with sharp needles inside for removing peas
holed by weevils, used by Messrs Sutton & Sons, Reading.

6 · Twenty-five widely grown Annuals and Biennials

Antirrhinum

Antirrhinum majus
The Common Snap-dragon

Scrophulariaceae
Europe

HISTORY. The ancestor of the garden antirrhinum came from the Mediterranean region and is a branching perennial plant growing 2–3 ft high with numerous spikes of flowers mostly crimson-magenta in colour but occasionally white.

TYPES. From this wild species, *A. majus*, have developed, mainly by natural variation within the species, several distinct garden forms. Tall: 3–4 ft; Intermediate: 2–2½ ft; Dwarf or Bedding: 1–1½ ft.

34. A fine bedding scheme of antirrhinums in a Buckinghamshire garden.

Latterly, crossing has taken place with other species such as *A. molle* and *A. glutinosum*, resulting in a race of dwarf growing plants of spreading habit with a wide range of colouring, known as Rock Hybrids, or Hybrid Gem.

COLOURS. Each section has now a wide range of colouring including white, cream, yellow, orange, shades of pink, orange-red, scarlet, crimson, and mauve. The plants remain in flower all summer.

USE. Tall varieties in the mixed border, placed among shrubs and herbaceous plants. Intermediate varieties in formal bedding and for growing in pots in the cool greenhouse where they are sometimes confined to a single stem. Both these sections are also excellent for cut flowers. Dwarf section for edgings and surrounding formal beds, also for patches in the rock garden where the rock hybrids are particularly valuable.

· CULTIVATION. Although strictly a short-lived perennial, best treated for garden purposes as a hardy or half-hardy annual. Sow seed in the open ground in July for flowering the following year, or in August under glass for wintering in cold frames, planting out in April or May. Usually, however, it is more convenient to sow the seed in a warm greenhouse in February or March and plant out into flowering quarters in May. For pot culture antirrhinums are best sown in August, grown quite cool and flowered on a single stem, one plant to a 5-in. pot. Although admirable for naturalizing on old walls and such like situations, to get the finest plants grow in well-cultivated soil in an open well-drained situation, but avoid fresh manure.

DISEASE: RUST. Some years ago gardeners were disturbed by an attack of a virulent form of rust, which much destroyed the value of antirrhinums for bedding purposes in the late summer and autumn. This seemed to develop most in the hotter and drier parts of the country. There are, fortunately, varieties available which are immune to this terrible disease. These are being developed, new colours being added rapidly, and are proving quite effective.

35. Tall antirrhinums.

China Aster

Callistephus chinensis   *Compositae*
China aster   China and Japan

HISTORY. Introduced from China in the early eighteenth century, the original plant was a branching annual about 2 ft high bearing single flowers with flattened purple ray florets.

TYPES. Since its introduction there have arisen forms with double flower heads, ray-petalled florets, incurved flowers, anemone-flowered, and so on. Instead of being confined solely to autumn, we can now have asters in flower from June to October and ranging in height from 6 in. to 3 ft, and with flowers ranging from miniature button-like flower heads to the large shaggy heads of the modern Californian varieties.

36. China asters, Dwarf Chrysanthemum-flowered.

Principal sections:

Double Giant: Ostrich Plume 18 in., Comet 18 in., Mammoth 2–3 ft, Californian Giant 2–3 ft.

Double Dwarf: Chrysanthemum-flowered 12 in., Miniature Pompon 12 in., 'Queen of the Market' 18 in. – extra early flowering.

Single: Single Sinensis 18 in., probably one of the best, useful for cutting and also for growing in drifts for naturalizing. An earlier more branching form is 'Southcote Beauty'.

COLOURS. The colour range is now so great that the China aster is one of the most valuable garden flowers. In most sections the colours include pure white, primrose, many shades of pink, scarlet, pale blue, mauve, purple, and dark blue.

USE. For cut flowers use both the single and double forms, especially those with long stems. These have a wide sale in florists' shops and last well in water. For bedding use all the varieties, either by themselves or in groups in the mixed border.

CULTIVATION. In the south of the country sow in the open ground about the end of April and early May, but for most gardens it is probably best to sow the seed in a cool greenhouse in March or April and plant out in May. A good rich well-cultivated loam suits asters best and they stand transplanting well. They also make excellent pot plants. They will stand slight shade and the single forms are suitable for naturalizing in open woodland.

DISEASES. Just after planting out, aphis is liable to attack the young plants and a precautionary spraying with an insecticide at this stage is advisable. Black neck and wilt can also be troublesome. The seedlings should be raised preferably in sterilized soil and planting in the same place two years running should be avoided. Spraying with bordeaux mixture or watering the young seedlings, during germination and up till planting out, with a 1–2 per cent solution of copper sulphate may also be recommended.

Fortunately varieties immune to the wilt disease have now been bred and as these become more generally available, should be grown more widely.

37. China asters, Ostrich Plume.

38. China asters, single.

Annual Chrysanthemum

Compositae

Chrysanthemum segetum. (Corn marigold) a native of our corn-fields and waste places, a beautiful plant so well known as hardly to need description.

Chrysanthemum coronarium. (Crown daisy) a native of S. Europe and introduced into this country over 250 years ago, a stronger growing plant than *C. segetum*, with very branching habit up to 3 ft in height, and more finely cut foliage.

Chrysanthemum carinatum. (Tricoloured chrysanthemum) a native of Morocco introduced about 150 years ago, about 2 ft high, the flowers being white with a zone of yellow at the base of the petals and dark chocolate-coloured centres, hence it was called *C. tricolor* at one time.

TYPES AND COLOURS. *C. segetum*, shades of yellow and ivory-white, having names such as 'Morning Star', 'Evening Star'; a particularly beautiful variety is known as 'Eastern Star' which, has a chocolate-coloured disc and primrose ray florets (Pl. 40). Height about 18 in.

C. coronarium. Considerably taller and more vigorous, shades of yellow and white. Particularly free flowering and vigorous, 2–3 ft high, flowering the whole summer through. A double form, 'Golden Crown' makes a good pot plant for the conservatory. The single yellow 'Golden Glory' is widely used as a cut flower for market.

C. carinatum. Rich crimson colours, some with double flowers (Pl. 39). A very good mixture of colours is usually offered under the name 'Eclipse'. The variety known as 'Burridgeanum' was the first to show the crimson colouring and an even deeper coloured form, 'Atrococcineum', is now available.

C. × spectabilis. Within the last year this new hybrid has appeared, raised by a well-known Swedish seed firm from a cross between *C. carinatum* and *C. coronarium*. Very vigorous, 3–4 ft, well branched and free flowering, in shades of yellow, primrose, and white, both double and single. This is a promising development. As an example of the length of time sometimes involved in

39. Annual chrysanthemum *C. carinatum*, single mixed.

raising a new variety of this sort, the original cross was made in the early 1920s and many thousands of plants were grown in the workshop over many years. Only in 1956 was it possible to offer the results for distribution to gardens.

USE. Its ease of cultivation and freedom of flowering make the annual chrysanthemum one of the most useful of hardy annuals in the garden. They flower over a long period and may be used in the annual border, in beds by themselves, or in the mixed border. The flowers last well in water when cut and they make excellent and easily grown pot plants for the cool greenhouse.

CULTIVATION. Easy; not fastidious as to soil; an open sunny situation suits them best. All perfectly hardy and may be sown in spring direct where they are to flower. Thin according to height and habit of growth. For pot culture in the cool house sow in September or October for flowering in spring and in spring to flower during summer.

40. Annual chrysanthemum *C. segetum* 'Eastern Star'.

Cornflower

Centaurea cyanus   *Compositae*
Cornflower   Europe, including the British Isles

HISTORY. A very old plant in our gardens and a well-known weed in our cornfields. The term 'cornflower-blue' is proverbial. The wild plant is upright and slender-growing, some 2 ft high with the well-known bright blue smallish heads of flowers.

TYPES AND COLOURS. From the original bright blue has sported a wide range of colours including white, pink, maroon, and purple. Many of these colours have been fixed and come true from seed. In addition there are the so-called 'double' forms, whose flower heads have an extra row of coloured florets, giving greater colour effect with larger flower heads, and therefore being better garden flowers.

A dwarf blue variety known as 'Jubilee Gem' arose in Essex just before the war and is useful for bedding. As the plants grow older, however, the rich blue effect is marred by the withered flower heads. There is also a dwarf pink variety.

USE. Mainly as a cut flower. The plants produce an abundance of flowers with long stems particularly if cut hard. From an autumn sowing flowers can be cut in April and with successive sowings in spring flowers can be cut all the season through.

CULTIVATION. The cornflower is one of the hardiest and easiest of hardy annuals to grow. In most parts of the country, seed may be sown in the open ground in August to October and will form bushy plants 3–4 ft high which should be thinned to 12 in. apart. Seedlings may also be transplanted in showery weather.

Aphis can be troublesome in the growing tips and should be guarded against.

41. Cornflowers, double mixed.

Dimorphotheca

Dimorphotheca   *Compositae*
Star of the Veldt, Namaqualand Daisy   South Africa

HISTORY. Dimorphothecas are slender-growing branching annuals bearing daisy-like flowers. The name Dimorphotheca is interesting, meaning Di=two, morphos=form, theca=box or seed vessel, i.e. bearing two forms of achenes or fruits; the disc florets bear the well-known flattened fruit whereas the ray florets bear rod-like corrugated fruits or 'seeds' quite distinct in appearance but producing an identical plant. The colour of the original plant is a light glowing orange and is usually known in gardens and seedsmens' catalogues as *D. aurantiaca*, but is probably nearer *D. sinuata* and *D. calendulacea*.

COLOURS. By hybridization, a wide range of colours is now available, including pure white, lemon, apricot, and deep orange, these being usually known as *D. aurantiaca* Hybrids. Those known as *Dimorphotheca* 'Special Hybrids' show trace of *D. pluvialis* influence, the colours being shades of reddish-purple

42. Dimorphotheca 'Sutton's Glistening White'.

43. *Dimorphotheca aurantiaca* 'Goliath'.

varied with tones of white, giving a quite unusual effect. A variety
of *D. pluvialis* known as 'Ringens' with a wide band of blue-
purple at the base of the ray petals is striking.

Use. Particularly valuable for growing in hot sunny borders. They provide delightful cut flowers for day-time decoration and flower over a long period in pots in the cool greenhouse. By successive sowing they will flower under glass during most months of the year.

Cultivation. In most parts of the country sow in a frame or cool greenhouse at the end of March or early April and plant out in May. The seedlings are easily transplanted. In light land in the south of England, they may be sown in place in the open ground in April. In good garden loam in full sun the plants flower freely the whole summer.

D. chrysanthemifolia, a half-hardy perennial, has very large clear yellow flowers borne on long stems, shown off well by the blue-green chrysanthemum-like foliage. This is best grown as a pot plant, sown in July and kept on a sunny shelf in the cool greenhouse. Stop once when 3–4 in. high to ensure breaking. Pot firmly in a good rich loam. Will flower the following April, May, and June.

D. ecklonis, a perennial shrub-like species, may be grown as an annual by being sown under glass in March and planted out in May. The bushy plants grow to a height of 2–3 ft bearing pure white flowers with a vivid blue disc, and are at their best in August and September. They look well in a mixed border and enjoy full sun. They are also useful as pot plants in the cool greenhouse. Hybrids between this species and *D. chrysanthemifolia* are offered. The flowers show a wide range of colouring, the habit being intermediate between the two species.

Eschscholzia

Eschscholzia californica   Papaveraceae
Californian Poppy   California

History. *E. californica*, the species most generally grown, is a somewhat variable perennial with a stout fleshy tap root, of a spreading habit, glaucous foliage, and light yellow flowers, found in dry sunny places in California.

89

44. Eschscholzia 'Aurora' and 'Fireglow'.

TYPES. Many varieties have been selected both for habit and colour, with both single and double flowers. Among the singles are taller varieties 12–18 in. high and a dwarfer and more compact-growing section about 12 in. high. The doubles are mostly dwarfer, 9–12 in. The colour range is now quite wide.

From the original bright yellow there arose a form with an orange zone at the base of the petals, then a pure self orange 'Crocea'. After that arose a more compact form with semi-double orange flowers. Then a gene was added giving an additional factor for the orange colour, resulting in the outer surface of the petals being bronze and the inner orange, 'Mandarin'; then a self bronze, and finally a rich orange-red and crimson. During the process, a rose-pink arose as a sport from the rich orange. Two of the more recent and probably the most distinct varieties in gardens today are 'Aurora', a creamy-pink, and 'Fireglow', a glowing orange, both with large beautifully shaped flowers (Pl. 44). There are also varieties with creamy-white and chrome-yellow flowers.

USE. With its recent development the Californian poppy has become one of our most showy garden flowers. It is not fastidious as to soil so long as the situation is well drained and sunny. It is most admirable for growing on hot sunny banks and will sow itself on old walls and such places. It can also be successfully used for cut flowers.

CULTIVATION. Although a true perennial, the eschscholzia is best treated in this country as a hardy annual, being sown in the open ground in March and April where it is to flower. It may also be sown with excellent results in autumn, in any well-drained, sunny position where winter frosts are not too severe. It will then come into flower in May and remain in flower the whole summer.

Another species *E. caespitosa* (*tenuifolia*) has much more finely cut foliage, is quite dwarf, with tiny flowers reaching a height of 6–8 in. and is very useful for growing in pockets in the rock garden and as edging. This is available in yellow and primrose. Another attractive species, *E. maritima*, has yellow flowers with an orange base to the petals and bright blue-grey foliage. It is charming in a hot sunny situation and, as it has a low-spreading habit, is also useful in the rock garden.

45. Eschscholzia 'Chrome Queen'.

Foxglove

Digitalis purpurea	*Scrophulariaceae*
Foxglove	Native in Great Britain

HISTORY. Our native foxglove is found in open woodland in light soils and has been long cultivated in our gardens. It is also used medicinally for the production of the drug digitalin. The wild plant is a biennial, rarely perennial, and the flower stems grow to a height of 2–3 ft or more, with pinkish-purple flowers.

TYPES AND COLOURS. Many of the garden forms have arisen by variation and selection. Crosses have also been made with other European species such as *D. lutea*. The result is that the colour range of this useful plant has been greatly extended. We now have pure white, primrose, pinks of various shades, apricot,

46. Foxglove, Sutton's Excelsior Hybrids.

and crimson. Many of these come quite true from seed. The white is particularly lovely in groups in the woodland where it can be caught in sunlight with a dark background. The primrose and apricot are both to be recommended. In mixtures beautiful intermediate shades are to be found, and in many cases the 'bells' are attractively spotted inside.

Recently a sport has arisen in America which has pure white flowers, borne all round the spike and carried horizontally. Crosses with this variety have produced a group known as Excelsior. The plants of this strain carry bold spikes of flowers reaching 5–6 ft in height with colours ranging from pure white, primrose, apricot-pink, and rose-pink to purple. The individual flowers are borne all round the stem horizontally, producing a striking effect. This strain may be used effectively in clumps in the mixed border or in beds in the open by themselves. They are quite distinct from the old-fashioned woodland plant from which they should be kept separate.

USE. Foxgloves are among the most useful plants for planting in light woodland and the semi-wild garden, where many of the newer colours available can be used to excellent effect. They can also be used as cut flowers. Foxgloves can be easily transplanted from the open ground in full bloom. A supply can therefore be grown in the reserve garden and lifted with roots, and transplanted wherever wanted, whether indoors or to other parts of the garden, when the plants will continue to open their flower spikes.

CULTIVATION. Sow in May or June in the nursery garden for flowering the following year. The seed is very fine, therefore sow thinly and only just cover. Transplant into nursery beds as soon as the seedlings can be handled and plant out into flowering position in autumn into a well-drained moist soil with abundant humus.

D. × *mertonensis* (*D. ambigua* × *D. purpurea*) is an unusual hybrid with dwarf-growing plants 12–18 in. high and with wide 'bells' of crushed strawberry colour. This is a short-lived perennial but will flower as a biennial.

94

Other species worth growing to flower as biennials are:

D. ambigua, spikes 2–3 ft with small yellowish flowers, mottled with brown.

D. orientalis, tall woolly spikes 3–4 ft, densely covered with small globular flowers with a prominent lip, off-white in colour with rusty reticulation, useful for unusual decorations and in the wild garden.

Godetia

Godetia	*Onagraceae*
Godetia	Western States of North America

HISTORY. The garden godetias have been derived from two American species, *G. grandiflora*, dwarf-growing, about 12 in. high with large flowers produced in clusters and *G. amoena*, taller and more slender growing, some 18 in. tall and with flowers in loose spikes. Colour is in both cases dull pink.

TYPES AND COLOURS. From *G. grandiflora* come most of the dwarf-growing garden varieties, ranging in height from 9 to 15 in. with a compact bushy habit and in colour from pure white through shades of pink to deep crimson. Later salmon-pink appeared, the first variety to be offered being 'Sybil Sherwood'. Richer coloured forms soon appeared, the best to date being 'Kelvedon Glory'. From *G. amoena* come the taller, looser growing varieties, with slender stems of flowers to a height of 2–2½ ft.

Doubles have also arisen in the Dwarf or Grandiflora section and are known as Azalea-flowered. These make a particularly bright show of colour, bearing plants 15–18 in. high and as much across, literally smothered in bloom, in colours of cerise-pink, bright crimson, and salmon.

From the hybridization of these two species a very popular section known as Tall Double has been developed. These produce tall vigorous-growing plants with long sprays of double flowers carried to the tips of the branches, very useful for cutting. The colours include white, shell-pink, rich pink, cherry-red, and crimson, all coming true from seed.

Two other kinds must be mentioned which are derived from different species. 'Lavender Gem', a distinct variety of loose slender habit with numerous flower spikes rising to a height of 15–18 in. The flowers are of medium size, pale lavender in colour with a clear white zone at the base of the petals. The prominent dark-coloured stamens show up well with the white base and are an added attraction to this beautiful variety, which probably comes from *G. viminea*.

G. dasycarpa from the Andes is a dwarf growing species with small mauve flowers and forms a compact plant 9 in. high with metallic green foliage. From this are derived the so-called blue and dwarf lavender and mauve varieties.

47. Godetia (Tall Double) 'Shell Pink'.

48. Godetia 'Salmon Princess'.

USE. A popular and very showy hardy annual. Owing to the long season of flowering and brilliant colours, very suitable for bedding, window boxes, and for cut flowers, especially the tall double varieties. The dwarfer growing varieties are quite suitable for a summer show in the rock garden. The flowers of the grandiflora section are delicately scented.

D

49. Godetia (Double Azalea-flowered) 'Salmon'.

CULTIVATION. Godetias give their best results in a well-cultivated soil in full sun. Sow in place as early in spring as is safe, i.e. whenever the land is working well and the air is genial, so as to get as long a season of growth as possible. Thin early and according to height. The tall double section is the hardiest and many be sown in place in the autumn in well-drained soil in an open favourable situation. They will then produce plants 3–3½ ft high and with long spikes of flower.

50. Godetia 'Lavender Gem'.

This section too provides striking pot plants for the cool green-house if sown at the end of September or early October, and potted on as required, flowering finally in 9- or 10-in. pots. When well grown these will provide plants 4–5 ft high, covered in flower by the end of May and early June. The important factors are to keep the plants under quite cool conditions, with just sufficient heat to keep out frost but no more, and abundant air and full light at all times. Use John Innes Potting Compost made with a fairly stiff loam for final potting.

Larkspur

Delphinium ajacis and
Delphinium consolida
Larkspur

Ranunculaceae

S. Europe

HISTORY. The garden larkspur is derived from two species of delphinium, *D. ajacis*, with blue, pink, or white flowers growing to 18 in., from which comes the Rocket or Hyacinth-flowered larkspurs, and *D. consolida*, slightly taller and with mainly blue flowers; this is the Stock-flowered or Imperial larkspur. Both species are found wild in Southern Europe, usually in cornfields and waste places.

TYPES AND COLOURS. Tall Rocket or Hyacinth-flowered is an early-flowering group and is usually offered in mixed colours. These include white, many shades of pink, mauve-purple, and blue. The colours blend well and make a very beautiful mixture. The plants grow about 3 ft, producing a single spike of double flowers. There is a Dwarf Rocket variety with similar colours and habit; height 1 ft.

The Stock-flowered and Imperial larkspurs are much more widely grown and form tall branching plants, 3–5 ft, and in a very wide range of colouring similar to that described for the Tall Rocket. Many colours can be obtained separately true from seed.

USE. Larkspurs are among the most useful of hardy annuals. They are extremely hardy and from an autumn sowing plants can be grown with spikes of flowers 5 ft or more, which besides forming handsome groups in the garden, are indispensable for cutting. The flowers last well in water, and owing to the wide range of colours available, are very popular. All the varieties, both tall and dwarf, are useful in the mixed border and for patches in the annual border where they make a display lasting over several weeks.

CULTIVATION. Larkspurs are not fastidious as to soil, and prefer an open, well-drained position especially for autumn sowing, where they will come through most winters successfully. Sow in August or September where they are to flower. The plants

51. Larkspur Stock-flowered, mixed.

grow up to 5 ft in height and the flowers appear towards the end of June and continue for 8–10 weeks. Sow also in March or April for flowering mid-July onwards. Look out for slugs, especially when the seeds are germinating, while in very severe weather birds may be troublesome.

When sowing in the cutting garden in autumn, sow moderately thinly and do not thin, unless the seedlings are much too thick, until genial weather in the spring when the plants may be simply singled to 2–3 in. apart in the row and say 2 ft from row to row. Each plant will then develop a tall single flower spike excellent for cutting and a great many stems will be produced from a small amount of space. In clumps in the garden proper, thin to 9–12 in. apart, to allow of further development.

Lobelia

Lobelia erinus   *Campanulaceae*
Lobelia   South Africa

HISTORY. The lobelia of gardens is a perennial of spreading habit in its native country, the colour of flowers varying from blue to pink or white.

TYPES AND COLOURS. The compact varieties of lobelia grow from 4 to 6 in. and many shades of colour come true from seed, thus avoiding the necessity of raising from cuttings, including white, pale blue, mid-blue, dark blue, purple, and crimson. There are also spreading and trailing varieties in similar colours.

USE. As long as lobelias have sufficient moisture, they will remain in flower the whole summer through and are therefore invaluable for bedding. A bed with all the colours available mixed together makes a striking sight. They are also useful as ground work with taller plants of contrasting colours planted among them, in patches in the rock garden, in window boxes, and in pots in the cool greenhouse.

CULTIVATION. As lobelia seed is so small, care must be taken in sowing. To ensure against sowing too thickly, a good way is to

52. Lobelia, dwarf compact.

measure out a small amount of seed according to the number of plants required, allowing a margin for accidents of course, and mix with sand before sowing. Seed should be sown in February or early March in heat and pricked out as soon as large enough, planting in the open towards the end of May and early June. Lobelias do best in a rich, well-cultivated soil which does not dry out. When grown in pots, they must never be allowed to become dry and when the plants come into flower, regular weekly doses of a good general fertilizer are beneficial.

L. tenuior (*ramosa*) which comes from Western Australia should also be treated as a half-hardy annual. It is of taller, upright habit, 10–12 in., with handsome bright blue flowers, and makes a beautiful pot plant.

Pot Marigold

Calendula officinalis   *Compositae*
Common or Pot Marigold   Southern Europe

HISTORY. The name is derived from 'calendae', the first day of the month, since it is found in flower nearly all the year round in sheltered places, particularly in its native habitat. The name *officinalis* means that the plant was used medicinally and in previous centuries was much used by herbalists. Even during the

103

recent war the flower heads were in demand by pharmacists. It is also used for flavouring soup hence the English name Pot Marigold.

TYPES AND COLOUR. As with so many composites, the original single-flowered plant with orange-coloured flowers has shown very wide variation in gardens. Varieties include 'Orange King' (Pl. 53), the best of the rich orange-coloured double forms, 'Frimrose Queen', and 'Apricot Queen'. Later there arose a taller growing form with long stems carrying loose-petalled double flowers giving an unusual shaggy effect which is quite attractive. This was named 'Chrysantha' or 'Sunshine'; there is also 'Radio' with globular, bright orange flower heads of quilled petals. Further varieties have been introduced recently from America, 'Pacific Apricot Beauty' and 'Pacific Lemon Beauty', both with long stems and good for cutting. Lastly 'Nova', a single orange with long petals and narrow dark chocolate-coloured centre with an extra long stem and lasting well in water, is well worth growing by those who prefer the single forms.

USE. One of the most accommodating of annuals, growing even in the poorest of soils and perfectly hardy. Also widely used as a cut flower and a most useful plant for the cool greenhouse, where it can be brought into flower all the year round.

CULTIVATION. In most southern parts of the country it may be sown in the autumn in an open, well-drained position, and unless the winter is extra severe it will come into flower by March. When sown in open ground it will flower from June to the end of the season. Besides doing well when sown in the place where they are to flower, the young seedlings can be transplanted without any difficulty in showery weather.

53. Pot Marigold 'Orange King'.

African and French Marigolds

Tagetes erecta, Tagetes patula   *Compositae*
African and French   Southern States of North
Marigolds   America

HISTORY. The African marigold, *Tagetes erecta*, is a native of Mexico and was first introduced over 300 years ago. The original plant grows to 2 ft and has single citron-yellow flowers, but like other composites, it has shown much variation under cultivation.

The French marigold, *Tagetes patula*, is a native of Mexico and South America. It is a dwarf-growing plant with brownish-yellow or mahogany flowers, also introduced over 300 years ago.

TYPES AND COLOURS. *The African Marigold.* Some twenty years ago the Giant Double varieties were probably the most popular and formed vigorous tall-growing plants with large globular heads of flowers up to 6 in. or more across in shades of yellow and lemon. There are also dwarf-growing varieties with similar heads of flowers, but all throw a percentage of singles.

Since then, and particularly recently, other variations have occurred, one of the most useful and beautiful being the Carnation-flowered, having double flowers, shaped more or less like a carnation. The first was 'Guinea Gold', brilliant orange, and throwing no singles. Other colours in this section are 'Primrose', 'Apricot' and 'Golden Yellow'. These form branching plants 2–3 ft high, covered with medium-sized flowers rather like a carnation in shape and with good stems for cutting.

Other recent variations are Chrysanthemum-flowered with shaggy heads resembling an incurved chrysanthemum flower, in lemon and yellow and orange shades, fully double. A very interesting group, Red and Gold Hybrids, raised from a cross between the African and French Marigolds, comes from America. As in many other inter-specific hybrids, this is intermediate in habit between the two species, forming bushy free-flowering plants 18 in. to 2 ft with medium-sized double flowers varying from red to orange; an attractive group but seed is still scarce.

The French Marigold. Many good garden varieties have been

54. Marigold, French (Dwarf Single) 'Lemon King'.

55. Marigold, French (Dwarf Double) 'Rusty Red'.

raised from this species, including singles and doubles. The plants are mostly dwarfer than those of the African marigold and literally covered in flowers. The colours range from palest lemon through yellow and orange to rich mahogany red, some being attractively marked with stripes and blotches.

Tagetes tenuifolia (*T. signata*) another species from Mexico and a most useful half-hardy annual. This forms bushy, free-flowering plants 12–15 in., covered with small single flowers, orange, yellow, and lemon. A form known as *pumila* is very compact and grows only 9 in. (Pl. 57), and is very useful for edgings and associating with both African and French marigolds.

USE. Since the new varieties are now available in both African and French marigolds, they have become most useful decorative plants. They thrive in hot sunny situations, but surprisingly appear to do equally well in dull wet seasons. This has been well proved recently. Both types remain in flower the whole season through, can be used in patches in the mixed border, in window boxes, for cut flowers, and in pots in the cool greenhouse.

CULTIVATION. The French and African marigolds are easily managed. It is important not to sow too early to avoid the plants having a check in the boxes, if they should be ready for planting out before the risk of frost is past. Do not sow before the end of March or early April in a cool greenhouse, sow thinly and prick out early. Plant out at the very end of May or early June when all risk of frost is over. Plant in an open sunny situation on well-cultivated ground.

An interesting form comes from Australia and is known as the Australian Tree marigold. If sown in the cool greenhouse in March, potted on as required, finally into 10-in. pots in a good compost, this will make a handsome, freely branched plant 5–6 ft high and 3 ft across with attractive foliage. The flowers resemble those of a double French marigold, red and orange in colouring, and appear in August and September. They may be placed out of doors on a sheltered sunny terrace in summer and make an unusual decorative plant for late August and September. When the pots becomes full of roots, they will benefit by regular feeding with an all-round fertilizer.

56. African and French Marigolds.

57. *Tagetes tenuifolia (T. signata) pumila.*

Nasturtium

Tropaeolum majus   *Tropaeolaceae*
Nasturtium   Mexico and South America

HISTORY. *Tropaeolum majus*, the original of our garden nasturtium, has been here for more than 300 years. Both by selection of natural variations and by hybridization with other species later introduced, such as *T. minus* and *T. peltophorum* (*T. lobbianum*) the well-known single garden nasturtium has been evolved. Later another variety with large fertile semi-double flowers, 'Golden Gleam', arose in Mexico and was introduced into this country from America.

58. Nasturtiums.

TYPES AND COLOURS. There are four main divisions of the
garden nasturtium today – Tall climbing single, Dwarf single
and the Semi-double Gleam varieties, which are semi-climbing in
habit with delicately scented flowers, and Dwarf Double. There
is a full range of colours in each section and these are very beautiful, including primrose, orange, salmon, orange-red, scarlet, and
deep mahogany, many of the flowers being beautifully marked
and spotted with contrasting colours. Most of the main colours
can be obtained separately true from seed.

USE. From the great diversity of habit, form, and colour of
flowers, coupled with ease of cultivation, it will be seen what a
valuable plant the garden nasturtium is. The tall varieties climb
by means of their soft green peltate leaves with long stalks, which
twist round their supports. They are beautiful sprawling over

rough sunny banks or over and through hedges or stumps of trees, or other supports. The Dwarf or Tom Thumb varieties are useful as edgings, in window boxes, and such situations. The semi-double Gleam section is probably now the most valuable in the garden. There are two types, the semi-tall and the dwarf or ball.

The flowers of all types are much used for cutting and whole sprays of the taller growing varieties can be used to show off the beautifully shaped leaves.

Under suitable conditions, the plants remain in flower the whole summer. Nasturtiums also make very attractive pot plants for the cool greenhouse and, by suitable sowings and with sufficient light, can be brought into flower at almost any season including mid-winter. For Christmas flowering, sow in August. The seedlings transplant easily.

CULTIVATION. This is of the simplest. Choose an open, not too rich, piece of land, and sow the seeds half an inch deep, about the end of April, where they are to flower. They will then not appear above the soil until risk of frost is over. The young seedlings will not stand any frost.

Black fly can be troublesome. Watch out carefully, and at the first signs spray with nicotine.

In difficult soils, nasturtiums may be sown in little pots in frames and planted out when conditions are suitable.

Canary Creeper. Tropaeolum peregrinum (*T. canariense*) is a more slender-growing plant than the climbing nasturtium, but it is an elegant climber, with prettily fringed golden-yellow flowers, which will flourish in either a shady or an open situation. It requires a richer soil than the other nasturtiums and from a late spring sowing will flower all summer.

Nemesia

Nemesia strumosa	*Scrophulariaceae*
Nemesia	South Africa

HISTORY. *Nemesia strumosa* was introduced to our gardens just over fifty years ago by Messrs Sutton of Reading. The wild plant

59. *Nemesia strumosa* var. *suttonii.*

is of straggly habit and is interesting in that the range of colouring of the flowers is quite a wide one, even in the wild. Another species also, *N. versicolor*, has been used in hybridizing to create the garden nemesia of today.

TYPES AND COLOURS. Probably the best variety is the Large-flowered form of *N. strumosa* var. *suttonii*, which is offered in a large number of separate colours coming true from seed, as well as in striking mixture. This has also been crossed with

113

N. versicolor, so that blue is now included in the range of colouring. This includes, beside a rich blue, white, primrose, yellow, orange, cherry-red, scarlet, and crimson. The habit is much more compact than in the wild plant, and the flowers larger, making the plant more decorative from a garden point of view; other varieties include 'Hybrid Blue Gem' – pale blue, 'Hybrid Aurora' – red and white bicolor, and Hybrid Mixed. The habit of this hybrid strain is more compact and bushy than *N. strumosa* and with much smaller flowers. In the mixture are many unusual shades. Another mixture worth growing is known as Triumph, which is really a dwarfer-growing strain of the large-flowered *strumosa*.

USE. Nemesias, owing to the brightness of their colouring, are one of our most widely grown half-hardy annuals. They make beautiful beds by themselves and as so many of the shades can be grown true from seed, beautiful contrasts and combinations of colour can be made. They are also useful for edging, for window boxes, and, especially the hybrid section, for patches in the rock garden. Since the flower buds open in water, the large-flowered nemesias are very good for cutting. Placed in low bowls, they make a beautiful table decoration, lasting sometimes 2–3 weeks in flower.

CULTIVATION. The nemesia is a typical example of a South African annual which requires cool moist conditions when young, and must on no account have a check in the early stage of growth. Therefore, do not sow the seed too early. Sow about mid-March under glass, keep cool, do not allow the seedlings to become dry and so arrange it that the young plants are ready for planting out, just when conditions are right. Nemesias prefer an open situation and a light, easily worked soil with sufficient humus. They make good pot plants for the cool greenhouse, flowering over a long period, and will flower at almost any month of the year by arranging the time of sowing. For example, sow in August for flowering at Christmas time, and September–October, for early spring. They also make admirable subjects for window boxes, but although they will make a brilliant display other plants must be ready to take their place as they do not last very long in such situations.

Petunia

Petunia　　　　　　　　　　　　　*Solanaceae*
Petunia　　　　　　　　　　　　South America

HISTORY. Garden petunias have originated from the crossing of
two South American species, *P. integrifolia* and *P. nyctaginiflora*.
These species were introduced into this country more than 100
years ago; from the hybrids many varieties have been selected,
showing much diversity of habit of plant, colour and size of
flower, and producing a most valuable race of garden plants.

Some readers may remember an interesting living demonstra-
tion of the origin of the garden petunia at Kew Gardens a few
years before the war, when the original species were shown, with
the results of their hybridization. It would be interesting to have
such living demonstrations revived.

60. Petunia 'Compact Pure White'.

61. Dwarf petunia 'Rose of Heaven'.

TYPES AND COLOURS. The present-day garden petunias can be roughly divided into three sections:

1. Large-flowered, which are best suited to cool greenhouse cultivation in this country.
2. Compact Single or Bedding (Pls 60 and 61) which as their name implies are the most useful for growing outside in beds and borders.
3. Double (Pl. 62), which are usually offered in mixed colours only and were originally raised in Japan, although seed is now produced in America.

The large-flowered or grandiflora section includes all the very large-flowered single varieties, many of which have ruffled and fringed flowers. The range of colours available from seed is quite a wide one, including white, shades of pink, red, crimson, pale

62. Double petunias.

blue, and violet, many with beautifully veined petals. A group with extra large flowers is known as Leviathan or Superbissima mixed. These are all best grown in pots under glass in this country. The compact single and bedding section has two divisions, the compact having a height of 9–12 in., and the bedding slightly taller in habit, mostly 15–18 in. The range of colours includes white, shades of pink, crimson, red, brilliant rose, mauve, violet, and blue, all coming true from seed, and when the season is a favourable one, continuing in flower the whole summer. Slightly taller-growing forms with spreading habit and single flowers, known as Balcony petunias, are very useful for growing in window boxes, on verandas, in stone vases, and in similar situations.

The doubles are usually offered in mixture only and are suitable both for pot and outdoor cultivation. Height 12–18 in.

USE. The single bedding petunia is one of the most valuable bedding plants we have, particularly for filling a warm sunny position. In such a situation in a favourable season it will continue in flower the whole summer. All the sections make excellent pot plants for the cool greenhouse, and the wide range of colours now available makes them very useful. Sometimes the single bedding varieties become too tall and straggling after flowering for some time in pots. They may then be cut hard back when they will break again and come into flower once more with renewed vigour.

CULTIVATION. A light, well-drained loam in a sunny situation suits petunias best. For pot cultivation sow seed in February under glass, pot on as required and finally singly into 5- or 6-in. pots. For outdoor bedding sow in March under glass, prick out into trays, and plant out when risk of frost is over, about early June. Here again do not sow too early and avoid giving the plants a check by having to hold them in the boxes too long before planting out.

...drummondii   *Polemoniaceae*
Phlox   Texas, New Mexico

. A variable rather straggly plant in the wild, varying
18 in. high and with purple and rose-coloured flowers
deeper eye. First collected by Thomas Drummond in
as, who sent the seed to England in 1835.

TYPES AND COLOURS. Today there are two main divisions –
the Grandiflora or Large-Flowered, 12–18 in. (Pl. 63). The stems
end in wide panicles of flowers of a very wide range of colours,
many of which come true from seed. These include pure white,
many shades of pink, vermilion, rich crimson, violet, and purple,
many with contrasting 'eyes'. There is also a variety *cuspidata* or
star with fringed flowers and pointed petals. The plants of the
other section are dwarf, compact, and very free flowering. The
best of these is a group called Beauty, characterized by large
flowers, a bushy, free-flowering habit, and a wide range of colours
which comes true from seed.

USE. One of the best of the half-hardy annuals. The large-
flowered section is very suitable for beds and borders and for
use as cut flowers since they last well in water and are delicately
scented. The compact forms are useful for edgings, window boxes,
and for formal bedding. If the plants are well grown, they will
flower the whole summer. They make excellent pot plants for the
cool greenhouse and for bringing into the house.

CULTIVATION. The annual phlox flowers best in a rich
calcareous soil with enough humus to conserve the moisture and
an open sunny situation. Sow in gentle heat in March and plant
out as early as is safe in May, if possible in showery weather. Try
to avoid any check in growth and if the weather becomes hot and
dry, watch out for thrips which can cause much damage. The
principle requirements are a good loam, cool conditions when
young, and full light when coming into flower. For pot culture
sow in August–September, pot on singly in 5-in. pots, and keep
on airy shelf during winter for flowering in April, May. Sow in

63. *Phlox drummondii.*

64. *Phlox drummondii* in border.

March to flower during the summer. Give abundant air and light at all times and do not allow to become dry. They will remain in flower the whole summer. The Beauty strain is particularly good for growing in pots, also a pure white variety known as 'Purity'.

Poppies

Papaver rhoeas	*Papaveraceae*
Corn Poppy	Europe including Britain

HISTORY. Our native corn poppy has long adorned our fields and gardens. It was from the wild scarlet poppy that the late Rev. W. Wilks made his world famous selections resulting in the production of the Shirley poppy about the year 1880.

TYPES AND COLOURS. The original selection of the Shirley poppies was a scarlet with a white edge and a white base. From this, Wilks gradually built up a beautiful strain showing a wide range of colours including white, pinks of all shades, including salmon, and many with attractive picotee edging, all with a white base. A fine mixture of double flowers is also available including all colours, and a mixture of slatey blue shades.

USE. Annual poppies are best seen in masses, either on the edge of a semi-wild part of the garden, in large groups in a mixed border, or grown in the cutting garden. The colours are delightful in mixture and the plants last for many weeks in flower, if not allowed to go to seed.

CULTIVATION. This is the simplest. An open situation on light, well-drained soil is best. They are very hardy and may be sown in September in the open, where they are to flower. They will stand as much as 20 degrees of frost and will flower from May onwards. For spring sowing, sow as soon as conditions will allow in March or April, when they will begin to flower in June. When cutting, select the flower buds just showing colour, place the ends of the stems in boiling water or a flame for a few moments to prevent the sticky juice from coagulating, and the flowers will last for several days in water.

65. Shirley poppies, Begonia-flowered, mixed.

66. *Argemone mexicana.*

DISEASES. Black fly is sometimes troublesome; keep a strict look-out and spray with nicotine at the first sign. A black stem rot sometimes appears at ground level especially in cold wet conditions. Remove diseased plants at first sign and dust ground with a colloidal copper dust.

OTHER POPPIES

Argemone mexicana. The Prickly Mexican poppy (Pl. 66), a native of Mexico, a handsome hardy annual 2 ft high with white or lemon-yellow poppy-like flowers and prickly foliage: it likes a hot sunny situation.

A. grandiflora, another Mexican species with bluish-green foliage without spines and glistening white flowers 2–4 in. across.

Glaucium flavum, the Horned poppy, deserves to be more widely grown in gardens, particularly in the semi-wild or natural garden. It is probably best treated as a biennial, seed being sown in the open ground in June. It forms a handsome plant 2–3 ft in height with medium-sized yellow and sometimes orange-red flowers and attractive glaucous green foliage. It is a native of our sea shores and will thrive in poor sandy soil, although it responds to better treatment.

Hunnemannia fumariifolia. The Mexican Tulip poppy, also deserves to be more widely grown in gardens. It grows 2 ft high, has an upright habit with finely cut foliage, blue-green in colour, resembling eschscholzia, and with very attractively shaped cup-like yellow flowers with long stems, good for cutting. It also makes a useful pot plant for the cool greenhouse and has the additional attraction of flowering in late summer, from July to September. It is probably best treated as a biennial and should be sown in a cold frame in August and planted out in spring in well-prepared soil with good drainage; it can also be treated as a hardy annual.

Papaver alpinum. The Alpine poppy, from the Alps and Carpathian mountains, although strictly a perennial, is best treated as a hardy annual or biennial. This is a diminutive poppy 6–8 in. high, the plants being covered with tiny flowers in pale pastel shades of white, pink, apricot, yellow, and orange. It does well in full sun and poor soil.

Papaver glaucum. The Tulip poppy, a charming annual from Asia Minor with spreading habit, blue-green foliage, and attractive pointed flower buds. The flowers are a shining red.

Papaver nudicaule. The Iceland poppy (Pl. 67), although a short-lived perennial from the northern sub-arctic regions, is always raised from seed and in fact can be flowered in one season by sowing under glass in the spring. It forms a pleasant tufted plant with light green foliage from which arise numerous dainty flowers on slender stems 12–18 in. long. The type plant is orange, but this has varied greatly and there is now a considerable range of colours, many of these coming true from seed. The colours, which are beautiful in mixture, include white, yellow, orange, pink, salmon, rose, and others with picotee edge, pale pink, and similar lovely pastel shades. The flowers last well in water, if the ends of the stems are charred in a flame. Sow in June

124

67. Iceland poppies.

and July, prick out into nursery lines 9 in. × 6 in. and plant into flowering positions in autumn for flowering the following year, when they will flower from May onwards. They can be planted in the mixed border, in the rock garden, and in the cutting garden. This is a good mixture known as Large-flowered, which has extra strong stems and large flowers. Double forms are also sometimes seen, but the single forms are the most decorative.

68. *Papaver somniferum*, double.

Papaver somniferum. Another very decorative poppy is the Opium Poppy (Pl. 68), a native of Greece and the Orient; an upright growing plant 2–3 ft with blue-green foliage and quite smooth stems. The garden forms are mostly double with very large flowers, extremely showy when at their best, and although rather short lived, are very good value when grown in clumps in a mixed border. Many colours can be raised true from seed, including a beautiful white, salmon-pink, and scarlet. Cultivation is very similar to that of *P. rhoeas*, although the opium poppy is not quite so hardy for autumn sowing.

Annual Scabious

Scabiosa atropurpurea	*Dipsaceae*
Sweet scabious, Pincushion Flower,	Southern Europe
Mournful Widow	

HISTORY. Introduced to our gardens about 300 years ago, the original scabious was a dull purplish-crimson and was much used in wreaths at funerals. Since then and particularly in the last twenty years a great improvement has been seen in the range of colours available, in the size of flower heads, and in the long stout stem useful for cutting.

TYPES AND COLOURS. The modern varieties known as Large-flowered produce vigorous growing plants with abundant flowers right through the season, on long stiff stems. A well-grown plant will grow 3–4 ft high and 18 in. across. There is now a wide range of colours which come true from seed. These include, white, many beautiful shades of pink, scarlet, pale mauve, blue, and dark maroon. A dwarf-growing strain 12–15 in. high with bushy plants in mixed colours is also offered.

USE. The sweet scabious can be used in clumps in the mixed border, in the cutting garden when flowers can be obtained all summer, and in pots in the cool greenhouse, both for summer and winter decoration.

CULTIVATION. It may be treated as a biennial or hardy annual. One of the best methods and well worth the extra

127

69. Annual scabious.

trouble, is to sow in early October in cold frames, prick out into trays in a good loam, keep quite hardy, only protecting during severe frost and plant out in March or April into flowering position. With such treatment, in a good garden loam, individual plants will grow 3–4 ft in height and as much as 18 in. across with 30–40 blooms open at one time. They will then come into flower at the end of June and continue till the autumn, giving abundant flowers for picking during all that time. Early and careful staking is advisable. Seed may also be sown in place in March or early April for flowering during the summer. For pots sow seed in June or July for winter flowering or in spring for flowering during the summer.

Schizanthus

Schizanthus	*Solanaceae*
Butterfly Flower, Poor Man's Orchid	Chile and Peru

HISTORY. The garden schizanthus have been derived from the crossing of two species, *S.grahami* and *S.pinnatus*, which were introduced to our gardens over 100 years ago. The name Schiz (to cut) and anthus (a flower), comes from two Greek words and refers to the finely cut petals of the flower.

TYPES AND COLOURS. The best known varieties for garden use come from the hybrid group and are known as Giant Hybrids or Large-flowered Hybrids. These produce vigorous branching plants 3 ft or more in height, covered with long trusses of flowers. These have a wide colour range and vary greatly, being attractively blotched and spotted, hence the name butterfly-flower. The colours include shades of pink, apricot, yellow, salmon, carmine, mauve, and purple, all in various combinations and markings. A variety known as 'Brilliance' is confined mostly to red shades.

A recent strain 'Gattleya Orchid' is unusual. The plants are very vigorous and the colours include shades of apricot, yellow, pink, carmine, mauve, and purple, many of the flowers, which are of good size, being strikingly veined and marked, rather like an old-fashioned chintz pattern.

E

A compact dwarf-growing group of similar colouring – Dwarf Bouquet – growing 12–15 in. is also offered.

Another group, Pansy-flowered, has been evolved recently. This has round flowers in self colours of pink, carmine-pink, lavender, mauve, and purple, and is most useful in definite colour schemes. The plants are not so strong growing in habit, reaching 18 in. to 2 ft.

USE. In favourable situations schizanthus can be sown under glass in March and planted out in May to flower in the open ground in June–July. The main use is, however, for pot culture in the greenhouse. With the diversity of colouring, quaint marking of the flowers, and freedom of flowering they make one of the most showy spring-flowering pot-plants for the cool greenhouse. They can also be sown in April for making useful colour in the greenhouse in August and September. The flower stems are excellent cut and last many days in water, the buds opening right to the tips of the branches.

CULTIVATION. For spring flowering under glass, sow in cool conditions in August, prick out singly into 3-in. pots, and grow on steadily, potting on as required, finally into 8- or 10-in. pots, if extra large specimens are wanted. Keep absolutely cool, giving abundant air and light. A John Innes Compost No. 2 is excellent for final potting with the addition of coarsely ground hoof and horn meal. Do not stop but allow the plant to break naturally. Early staking is advisable, giving extra staking as required. When the pots are full of roots, the plants will profit from gentle feeding with liquid manure. Sow again in April to flower on a single stem in a 5-in. pot in August. This is the time of year when they are very useful for indoor decoration and as cut flowers. Schizanthus can also be sown in gentle heat in March and planted out into a sunny sheltered position in May as a half-hardy annual.

70. A well-grown plant of schizanthus.

Stocks

Matthiola   *Cruciferae*
Stocks or Gilliflower   Europe including Britain

HISTORY. Stocks have been grown for many years in British gardens and are the 'gilliflowers' of Shakespeare's day. Most of the garden stocks have been derived from the European *Matthiola incana*, a woolly grey-leaved plant of biennial and sometimes perennial character. Annual forms of this species have also arisen from which come the Ten-week Stock and other annual forms of garden stocks, whereas the Brompton or spring-flowering stock comes from the biennial form. Another species, *M. sinuata*, also comes from Europe and is occasionally found on our coasts. It is the parent of the Intermediate or East Lothian Stocks.

TYPES AND COLOURS. For garden purposes, stocks may be divided into four classes – the spring-flowering Brompton stocks, and three classes of the annual forms; summer, autumn, and winter-flowering.

Spring-flowering or Brompton stocks. Brompton stocks (Pl. 71) are hardy biennials, forming branching plants 12–18 in. high and flowering freely in May and June. There is a wide range of colours which come true from seed, including various shades of pink, carmine, mauve, purple, and white. In favourable situations, particularly near the sea on chalk, Brompton stocks sometimes survive over several years and reach a height up to 5 ft; when covered in flower in the spring they make a handsome sight. A variety of Brompton stock, 'Empress Elizabeth', bright carmine rose, is especially good for flowering under glass during winter.

Summer-flowering ten-week. The first of the summer flowering stocks. The best strain is that known as Giant Perfection (Pl. 72), with strong growing, free flowering, branching plants up to 18 in. and in a wide range of colours including white, yellow, many shades of pink, crimson, pale mauve, blue, and purple. Bedding strains of dwarfer habit are also offered and a strain known as Giant Rocket or Column, in which each plant produces

132

71. Stock, Brompton.

one long spike of bloom 2 ft high, is particularly good for cutting.

Autumn-flowering stocks. The best is the East Lothian, of which, from a spring sowing, the plants come into flower in July and August. The dwarf bushy plants grow to a height of 1 ft and have a wide range of colouring. They will also flower in the cool green-house in early spring from a July or August sowing.

Winter-flowering stocks. The best is the Beauty of Nice strain, forming vigorous branching plants in a very wide range of colouring. These will flower from Christmas onwards.

Wallflower-leaved stock. A variety with smooth green leaves known as Wallflower-leaved 'All the Year Round' is also excellent for growing in pots, during early spring. The pure white flowers are admirably set off by the shiny deep green foliage.

All stocks throw double and single flowers, and although the single forms are very beautiful and quite useful as cut flowers, the double are usually preferred and of course last longer. Seed is only produced by the single-flowered plants, therefore to have doubles one must grow a race carrying the factor for doubling. This is a genetical factor and can only be guaranteed to approximately 50 per cent. In recent years a new race has been evolved in Denmark known as Hansen's 100 per cent Double. The factor for doubling has been linked with the colour of the cotyledon. It is possible therefore, by pricking off the seedlings with pale green cotyledons, to have 100 per cent doubles, the dark green being the singles. These seedlings must always be raised in cool conditions otherwise the difference in colour of the cotyledon is less well marked.

Ten-week, Column, and Beauty of Nice groups are all available in this race.

USE. Stocks in all their forms are among the most valuable of all garden plants for decoration. In the mixed border, in beds by themselves, and in the cutting garden, they give colour and fragrance during spring, summer, autumn, and under glass in winter. By correct use of sowing times and choice of suitable varieties, they can thus be of value in gardens throughout the year.

CULTIVATION. All stocks should be grown in rich, well-cultivated soil, with good drainage and abundant light. They should never lack for moisture in the summer and should have sufficient lime to make the soil alkaline. Prick out young seedlings quite early in the cotyledon stage.

Brompton. Sow in July in cold frames. Prick out into trays or, if possible, singly into 3-in. pots, plant out into flowering

134

72. Stock, Giant Perfection.

quarters by end of September or early October to give them time to be well established before the winter. Should there be a risk that conditions are too wet in winter or frost too severe, a number should be potted on and kept in cold frames for protection and planted out in early spring. The autumn-planted always make the best plants if they survive.

Summer-flowering. Sow under glass in March thinly and prick off as soon as the seedlings can be handled. They may be pricked off into trays or direct into cold frames in good soil; as soon as they are established give all air and light possible. Plant out as soon as ready so as to avoid any check.

Autumn-flowering or East Lothian. Similar treatment is suitable except that they should be sown at end of February or early March. These may also be sown in August for wintering under glass in pots, coming into flower in early spring.

Beauty of Nice or Winter-flowering. Sow in June thinly in shallow boxes and prick off into small pots. Grow on in cold frames and pot on as required in a good compost to which some mortar rubble has been added. Bring into the greenhouse at the end of October or November. When the flower trusses are formed weak liquid manure may be given. Beauty of Nice stocks may also be sown under glass in March for planting out in the open border in May. When planted at 12 in. apart they give a wonderful display of flower during the summer months and are also most useful for cutting.

Sunflower

Helianthus annuus	*Compositae*
Sunflower	Western United States

HISTORY. The common sunflower was introduced into this country over 300 years ago and is a valuable economic plant in many parts of the world. Valuable oil is produced from the seeds, which are also useful for food; the leaves are used for fodder and the flowers yield a yellow dye.

TYPES AND COLOURS. The giant annual yellow sunflower is a tall coarse-growing plant reaching 8 ft in good soil. Many

73. Sunflower 'Sutton's Autumn Beauty'.

varieties have appeared in gardens including some with 'double' flowers, which are unattractive. An interesting variation which appeared in California in 1910 has chestnut-red markings in the ray petals. This was developed by Messrs Sutton of Reading and finally offered under the name of 'Sutton's Red'. By crossing, other varieties were produced including a chocolate-coloured self and a wine-red.

Another species, *H. debilis* (syn. *H. cucumerifolius*), has freely branched plants 3–4 ft high and 2–3 ft across with numerous small yellow flowers and glossy green leaves shaped somewhat like a cucumber leaf. These are sometimes known as Miniature sunflowers. A variety named 'Stella' with long golden ray petals and dark narrow centres is one of the best.

Recently a cross between this variety and the red sunflower has been offered with the name of sunflower Sutton's Autumn Beauty. Thus has arisen a very attractive garden plant, 4–5 ft high, freely branching and with long flower stems. The flower heads have long ray petals with small centres and the colours are quite remarkable, ranging from pale primrose through orange-yellow, bronze, chestnut brown, and maroon, many very beautifully marked.

USE. The ordinary giant sunflower is not a plant of artistic merit in a garden, but may be useful as a screen and sometimes a row of their giant heads topping a garden wall or hedge has a certain appeal. The smaller growing miniature sunflowers and their hybrids with their branching habit, smaller leaves, and slender flower stems make very useful garden plants both for growing in the mixed border and for cut flowers.

CULTIVATION. All the sunflowers are of easy culture, not being fastidious as to soil, but requiring light and air. Sow in place about the end of April, also in boxes or small pots mid-April and plant out towards the end of May. They transplant easily.

Sweet Pea

Lathyrus odoratus   *Leguminosae*
Sweet Pea   Sicily

HISTORY. The sweet pea with its many forms and varieties demands a book to itself and in fact many books have been written on it, tracing its fascinating development in our gardens.

This is undoubtedly one of the most useful and widely grown of annuals. The story of its development from the rather insignificant wilding from Sicily, seeds of which were received in this country in 1699, to the present-day modern varieties, is one of the most fascinating in the history of the development of garden flowers. The original was a slender-growing climbing plant with small, sweetly scented reddish-purple flowers. Some forty years after its introduction two sports appeared, a white variety and a red and white bicolor known as 'Painted Lady'. Further colour forms appeared some sixty years later, but it was not until about 1880, when Henry Eckford first started crossing, that larger flowers and greater variety of colour appeared. The dwarf or Cupid variety also appeared in America in the year 1893, and later in this country. But by far the most outstanding mutation to appear was the large-flowered wavy-petalled variety finally named 'Countess Spencer' in whose garden it had appeared in 1900. This same variation appeared in other gardens during the same year. This led to a wave of inter-crossing by many enthusiastic gardeners and seedsmen, resulting in the creation of the many fine varieties of the present time, with their wide range of colouring, and large flowers with long flower stems.

TYPES. Another valuable race is that of the Early-flowering or Winter-flowering sweet pea. These appear to have arisen as a sport from the normal flowering sweet peas and arose in America, Australia, and Algeria, hence at one time were named Algerian sweet peas. They are characterized by flowering several weeks earlier than normal sweet peas, but make a more slender plant with small flowers. It is interesting to notice that in all three countries, the climate is hotter than in England. The Early-flowering strain has always shown to much better advantage under hotter climate conditions than here and is most useful in this country when grown under glass. By sowing early in the autumn, the plants can be brought into flower from Christmastime onwards.

Recently there has come from America a new race known as Cuthbertson sweet peas. This arose from a cross between the existing strain of early-flowering and the normal or late-flowering strain and appears to combine the good qualities of both strains. This strain comes into flower some 2–3 weeks earlier than normal sweet peas and has large flowers and vigorous growth. It has become very popular in America and is proving useful for growing under glass in this country.

Other forms are still appearing, such as that known as Multiflora, also raised in America, bearing 5–7 flowers to a stem and very vigorous. A large-flowered, frilled Dwarf Cupid group was introduced from America in 1956 called Little Sweetheart.

There are thus now six distinct strains of Sweet Peas:

The Giant Frilled or Spencer.
The Early-flowering (winter) Frilled.
The Cuthbertson (spring-flowering) Frilled.
The Multiflora.
The Dwarf Cupid.
The Dwarf Cupid Giant Frilled (Little Sweetheart).

USE. The first use of sweet peas is undoubtedly as cut flowers. Their wide range of colouring which includes practically every colour except yellow, their delicate scent, and long season of flowering make them one of the best cut flowers for the garden. Owing to the wide range of colours available, which come true from seed, all kinds of beautiful blends and contrasts of shades can be arranged to suit every taste. Planted in clumps of, say, 5 or 6 plants in the mixed border, when neatly staked, sweet peas are very decorative. A hedge of mixed colours in the kitchen garden or alongside a path can be a delightful feature of the garden in addition to providing cut flowers. The modern system of growing on single stems and disbudding will certainly give larger flowers and longer stems superior for cutting, but an old-fashioned hedge of sweet peas is a much more satisfying sight in the garden.

74. Sweet pea, a modern variety.

The dwarf cupid varieties, especially the new Little Sweetheart, make telling patches of colour in the front of the mixed border and are useful as edgings.

CULTIVATION. Sweet peas amply repay thorough cultivation of the soil. To get good results it is now hardly considered necessary to go several feet deep in making special trenches but rather it is found better simply to double dig the whole plot where the sweet peas are to be grown and give the necessary organic manure. Sowing is best done in October in cold frames and the seedlings potted on singly when ready, keeping perfectly hardy in cold frames all winter, only protecting in the case of severe frosts.

Plant out as early as the weather is genial in March into flowering position. The methods for growing for exhibition, training on the cordon system, and so on are best learnt from books specially written for the purpose.

Verbena

| *Verbena* × *hybrida* | *Verbenaceae* |
| Verbena | South America |

HISTORY. Garden verbenas have arisen from the inter-crossing of various South American species and, although strictly speaking perennials, are best treated as half-hardy annuals. In the old days verbenas were always propagated by cuttings taken in the spring, but the great improvement in seedling strains both in trueness to colour and compactness of habit renders this unnecessary.

TYPES AND COLOURS. Modern strains of verbena form compact bushy plants 12–15 in. high and as much across and have a very wide range of colours, white, shades of pink, mauve, purple, and rich blue, mostly coming remarkably true from seed. The finest are the Large-flowered or Mammoth section. There is also a Dwarf compact strain 9 in. in height with small flower heads and a full range of colours. Flowering begins in June and lasts until stopped by frosts in autumn. Three other species may be mentioned:

75. Verbena, a large-flowered variety.

V. tenuisecta (*erinoides*). Moss verbena, with finely cut foliage, mauve flowers, and spreading habit, very free flowering, 6–9 in. There is also a white form.

V. rigida (*venosa*). A hardy perennial, very useful for bedding when grown as a half-hardy annual, and with small spikes of violet-purple flowers, flowering the whole summer, 1 ft. Particularly useful near the sea.

V. bonariensis. A tall hardy perennial growing 3–4 ft with rosy purple heads of flowers, rather a coarse plant but useful for massing in the semi-wild garden, and for cutting. Easily treated as a H.H.A.

USE. Owing to their wide range of colouring and long period of flowering, from the end of June until September, verbenas are among the most useful bedding plants. Many varieties are sweetly scented, 'Large-flowered Blue' being especially strong. The compact varieties are also good for window boxes, edgings, and patches in the rock garden, also for growing in pots. They stand hot sunshine particularly well.

CULTIVATION. Verbenas should be sown under glass in February, pricked out into trays as soon as fit to handle, hardened off in cold frames, and planted out in May. They prefer a rich, well-drained loam and love sunshine with sufficient moisture in the early stages of growth.

Thrips are apt to be troublesome, so much so that a preventive spraying with nicotine or other convenient insecticide is often advisable in the early stages after planting out.

Wallflower

Cheiranthus cheiri	*Cruciferae*
Wallflower	Europe (naturalized in Britain)

HISTORY. The wallflower was very early introduced to this island from Europe where it quickly became naturalized on old walls, in fact, a bushy small-flowered yellow variety, 'Old Castle', was offered for many years for naturalizing, but unfortunately appears to have been dropped from seed lists.

TYPES AND COLOURS. The latest development is undoubtedly the Giant strain. When well grown, this will produce vigorous bushy plants, each carrying many handsome spikes of flowers, 18 in. or more. The range of colour now available is remarkable, the most outstanding being 'Giant Fire King', a flame red; other colours include primrose, several shades of yellow, brown, blood-red, crimson, pink, and ruby. Among the smaller-flowered varieties 'Purple Queen' is a good cool purple, useful for associating with the pale primrose varieties.

The early-flowered section is a great improvement on the old annual Parisian Wallflowers. Sown at the usual time these varieties come into flower several weeks earlier than the giant-flowered varieties. In fact in sheltered positions, say on the south coast, varieties such as 'Early-flowering Phoenix' and 'Early-flowering Yellow Phoenix' will in a favourable season come into

76. Giant wallflowers.

full flower regularly by February. These varieties are also widely grown in Cornwall for early cut flowers for the market.

The double wallflowers, both the tall and the dwarf-branching are well worth growing, especially in pots in the cool greenhouse for winter decoration.

USE. Wallflowers are very widely grown for spring bedding and for cutting. The wide range of colouring and their delicious scent make them invaluable for spring bedding. A patch in a sheltered bed under a window where the scent can be wafted into the house should always be arranged when possible. All the varieties and especially the early-flowering section are especially useful for growing in pots in the cool greenhouse.

CULTIVATION. Wallflowers require an open sunny situation and do best in a soil containing sufficient lime. Sow in a nursery bed in May and June, prick out in showery weather in nursery lines 12 in. by 9 in. and place into flowering position as soon as the soil is moist enough in October.

Should space be available, seed may also be sown in the open ground in early July and thinned out in, say, two operations, to 12–15 in. apart to flower where they stand. These may be especially useful in the cutting garden and also in places in the mixed border.

Mention should also be made of the following:

Cheiranthus kewensis, the result of crosses made at Kew between *C. semperflorens* (*mutabilis*) and forms of *C. cheiri*; *C. kewensis* makes a most valuable fragrant winter-flowering plant for the cool greenhouse, 1 ft high, flowers mauve in bud, opening to primrose-yellow, fading to pale purple as the flowers go over. Seeds sown in July will provide a show of colour for many months in winter.

Cheiranthus × allionii, the Siberian Wallflower, probably an *Erysimum* hybrid, raised by Mr John Marshall of Limburn in 1846. This is best treated as a biennial and is very free-flowering, 15 in., bearing trusses of bright orange-coloured flowers in May; it may be sown in July and August in the open ground where it is to flower.

Zinnia

Zinnia elegans   *Compositae*
Zinnia – Youth and Old age   Mexico

HISTORY. The original species, *Z. elegans*, from which the large-flowered garden forms of zinnia have been developed, has single flowers of purple or lilac with a yellow centre. It is a very variable species and it is mainly during the last 40–50 years that the wide range of variation has been obtained by selection.

TYPES AND COLOURS. The most recent strains have been developed in America where the zinnia is a very popular flower. The largest of the doubles is the Giant Dahlia-flowered, producing robust plants 2–3 ft in height and immense double flowers up to 5 in. across in a wide range of colouring, many distinct colours coming true from seed. These include primrose, golden-yellow, orange, salmon-apricot, pink, scarlet, crimson, lilac, and purple. A similar strain known as Mammoth has an equally wide range of colouring. Another strain known as Chrysanthemum-flowered bears heads of flowers with incurved petals after the appearance of a chrysanthemum. One of the best of this type is 'Burpees Hybrid'.

Miniature Pompon Mixed or Lilliput has dwarf bushy free-flowering plants, 9–12 in., bearing fully double miniature flowers with a wide range of colouring including orange, salmon, scarlet, golden-yellow, lilac, and white (Pl. 78).

Another dwarf bushy species, *Z. haageana* (Pl. 79), is also well worth growing; 9–12 in., with single and semi-double flowers in a wide range of colours, many of the ray petals being tipped with yellow and lemon with a broad zone of chocolate maroon at the base.

USE. The modern zinnia is one of the most brilliant coloured of all annuals. Zinnias are widely grown for cut flowers and last well in water. When the conditions are suitable, they are admirable grown in beds or in patches in the mixed border. They also make good plants under glass especially when grown on single stems for cutting. The dwarf-growing strains are very suitable for edgings and window boxes. They have the added

77. Giant zinnias.

78. Zinnia, 'Miniature Double' or 'Lilliput'.

quality of standing up to adverse weather conditions better than the large-flowered strains. They are also attractive as cut flowers and for making the tight bouquets and bowls beloved of the Victorians.

CULTIVATION. Zinnias revel in a rich soil with moisture, and hot strong sunshine. They resent transplanting and must on no account receive a check when young. Therefore do not sow before April and preferably prick off direct into 3-in. pots, planting out into a warm sunny position in showery weather in early June. Seed may also be sown in the open in May in rich, well-prepared ground, which is often quite a satisfactory method. Sow the seed in little clumps 9–12 in. apart and thin to one plant per clump.

For flowering under glass, sow in October in small pots and pot on as required for stocks. With a final potting into 8- or 9-in. pots they will make plants 4 ft high and remain in flower for months. They may also be sown direct in the soil border in the greenhouse in early spring where they will be very successful for cut flowers.

79. *Zinnia haageana.*

7 · General descriptive list of Annuals and Biennials

Abbreviations: H.A. Hardy Annuals; H.H.A. Half-hardy Annuals; H.H.P. Half-hardy Perennials

Acroclinium: see **Helipterum.**

Adonis: Pheasant's Eye; Europe; *Ranunculaceae.*

A. aestivalis. H.A. from Central Europe. Suitable for mixed borders, patches in rock garden, and open woodland or wild garden planting, also for cutting. 1–1½ ft, branching plant with deep green finely cut foliage, small deep crimson buttercup-like flowers about 1 in. across. Flowers June or July. Sow in spring or autumn.

Agathaea coelestis: see **Felicía amelloides.**

Ageratum: Central America; *Compositae.*

Derived from *A. conyzoides* and *A. houstonianum (mexicanum).* From these have been bred many useful garden forms varying from 6 to 18 in. The dwarf forms are very useful for bedding,

80. Ageratum 'Little Blue Star'.

151

forming compact growing plants covered with fluffy heads of flowers varying in colour from pale lavender to deep mauve (Pl. 80). The taller forms make good cut flowers. Ageratums prefer a warm sunny situation and will flower throughout the summer months. They also make good pot plants for the cool greenhouse. Sow in March under glass; plant out end of May.

Agrostemma: Europe and Western Asia; *Caryophyllaceae.*

A. 'Milas', a form of *A. githago*, our native corn-cockle, is one of our most beautiful hardy annuals (Pl. 81). It was found near the town of Milas in Turkey, hence the name. A graceful, slender growing plant 2–3 ft high with large viscaria-like flowers, 2–3 in. across, pale lilac in colour. In spite of its slender habit the plant stands up well to wind and wet, and with its long narrow foliage makes a most useful cut flower. It may be sown in autumn or spring, and is of the easiest culture. A good subject also for the mixed border and for the annual border.

Alonsoa: Chile and Peru; *Scrophulariaceae.*

Alonsoas delight in a light rich soil and an open situation. They are quite easy to grow and will flower over a long period. They are best treated as H.H.A., sown in gentle heat in March, and planted out at the end of May and early June. They appear to be remarkably indifferent to weather, flowering well either in a wet season or dry. One of the best is *A. warscewiczii*, of bushy habit and small bright green leaves, the stems in summer being covered by small scarlet flowers. Height 18 in. There is a compact form 9–12 in. and a soft pink form sometimes offered under the name of *A. mutisii*. They all make charming pot plants for the cool greenhouse, flowering over a long period.

Althaea: Hollyhock; Orient; *Malvaceae.*

A. rosea. Handsome perennial garden plants. Many named varieties were at one time grown but owing to the devastating hollyhock rust these have greatly died out. Hollyhocks are therefore mostly grown from seed nowadays and are easily raised by sowing seed in the open ground in nursery lines in June or July. Plant out into their flowering positions in early autumn unless the winters are extra severe, when they should be given the protection of a frame. They will flower the following June and July, the handsome flower spikes growing to a height

81. *Agrostemma githago* 'Milas'

of 8–9 ft. Double and single-flowered forms are available in many shades of colour including pure white, pink, rose, yellow, apricot, and crimson (Pl. 82). Hollyhocks appear to thrive in the neighbourhood of towns where attacks from the deadly rust appear much less frequent. Annual forms are also available and from a sowing under glass in February and March, plants will flower from July onwards, the flower spikes up to 4–5 ft. Double and single strains are available in a wide range of colours.

Alyssum: Europe and W. Asia; *Cruciferae*.

A. maritimum (*Lobularia maritima*). The Sweet Alyssum of gardens, a most useful hardy annual. This forms a low-growing spreading plant with narrow grey foliage up to 12 in., freely branched, each branch ending in a spike of small usually white flowers, sweetly scented and much loved by bees. Useful as edging, on walls and rock gardens. There is a very compact growing form, known as 'Minimum' which makes a dense low-growing carpet of flowers, very useful for placing among stones on a terrace or growing over a wall. There are also lilac-coloured forms.

A. saxatile. A grey-leaved sub-shrub, perennial but easily flowered as a biennial. Flower spikes rich yellow and a most useful spring flowering plant for the rock garden or wall. Easily raised from seed sown in April and May, for flowering the following spring. There is an attractive pale lemon form known as 'Silver Queen'.

Amaranthus: Love-lies-bleeding, Prince's Feather, Joseph's Coat; Tropics; *Amaranthaceae*.

Some useful species of garden annuals are included in this genus and have been grown in English gardens since Tudor times. Some, such as *A. caudatus*, the well-known Love-lies-bleeding (Pl. 83), and its so-called white or rather pale green form, are useful for cutting especially when stripped of their leaves; with *A. hypochondriacus* (Prince's Feather) these may both be treated as hardy annuals growing to a height of 2–3 ft. Other species should be treated as H.H.A. They all delight in a warm soil and sunny situation with sufficient moisture. There is a danger of the plants becoming too coarse if the soil is too rich.

154

82. *Althaea*. Double hollyhocks.

A. tricolor (*melancholicus*) (Joseph's Coat) is a valuable foliage plant and particularly the form *splendens*, which has leaves of a rich scarlet-crimson marked with yellow and bronze-green. Height 18 in. *A. tricolor ruber* has bright red ornamental foliage, height 12 in., and *A. salicifolius* has long undulating foliage brilliantly coloured with orange, carmine, and bronze, height 3 ft. All are also useful for pot cultivation.

Anagallis: Pimpernel; Western Mediterranean; *Primulaceae*.

The Scarlet Pimpernel of our fields is a well-known charming plant. The kinds usually grown in the garden, however, are forms of *A. linifolia*, sometimes listed as *grandiflora* or large-flowered, and include the bright red (*parksii*) and the deep blue (*phillipsii*). These, although perennial in their native state, are best treated as H.H.A. in gardens. Both forms make compact free-flowering showy plants 6–8 in. high, very suitable for the annual border, for edging and patches in the rock garden. In a warm sunny position they will flower for most of the summer.

Anchusa capensis: Alkanet; South Africa; *Boraginaceae*.

The annual forms grown in gardens come from the South African *Anchusa capensis*, biennial in its native country. They succeed best as hardy annuals here. The variety 'Blue Bird' is probably the best (Pl. 84) making compact free-flowering plants 15–18 in. high and when well grown 12 in. across, with bright blue flower heads resembling forget-me-nots. 'Bedding Bright Blue' with azure blue flowers is also attractive.

Among the perennial forms the well known *Anchusa italica* (*azurea*) from the Caucasus can be very successfully grown as a biennial. Sow in April in nursery lines in the open ground and plant into flowering positions in autumn. An open sunny well-drained position suits them admirably and they look best when planted in large drifts in the semi-wild garden. The original plant was somewhat straggly in habit, growing to 5 ft. Modern strains have been developed with a more compact habit and larger flowers. The colour also has been much improved and we now have, besides the well-known 'Drop-more', 'Morning Glory', one of the best, and 'Pride of Dover', azure. Several strains remarkably true from seed are offered in these shades and are well worth growing.

156

83. *Amaranthus caudatus*
(Love-lies-bleeding).

84. Anchusa 'Blue Bird'.

157

Anthemis arabica: see **Cladanthus arabicus.**

Antirrhinum: see Chapter 6.

Aquilegia: Columbine; Europe, North America; *Ranunculaceae.*
Although strictly perennials, the hybrid strain known as Long-spurred Hybrids (Pl. 85) is best raised from seeds and if purchased from a reputable source can be grown in a very wide range of delightful colours. Various shades of colour such as blue-shades, pink, yellow, white, and so on will come quite true from seed. They make charming plants for the mixed border and for cutting.

In the south of England, seed is best sown in September and kept in cold frames until the following spring when the young seedlings may be pricked out into nursery lines in beds where they may be shaded in the initial stages until the little plants are fully established. Plant into flowering position in early autumn. A good loam with enough lime to make it slightly alkaline and with moisture suits them best.

Arctotis: African Daisy; South Africa; *Compositae.*
The intercrossing of several species of Arctotis, natives of South Africa, has led to the creation of a most valuable strain of great decorative value, namely *Arctotis* Special Hybrids or Large-flowered Hybrids (Pl. 86). These produce vigorous growing plants with attractive grey foliage, above which arise the large flower heads on stalks 15–18 in. long. The daisy-like heads open in daylight 3–4 in. across and have a very wide range of colours including white, pink, bronze, rich red, crimson, cream, yellow, orange, and wine shades, many with beautiful contrasting zones of colour at the base of the ray petals. They provide excellent cut flowers for day-time decoration. These hybrids are of quite easy culture, doing best in a good loam, in an open sunny situation, planted out in the open about the middle of May from a sowing under glass in early March. The plants will come into flower in June and continue until cut down by frost in autumn. Like so many South African annuals they do not like to be too dry at the roots especially in the early stages.

Arctotis grandis is another species well worth growing in the garden. Raise in gentle heat in March and plant out in May,

85. Aquilegia, Long-spurred Hybrids.

86. Arctotis, Suttón's Special Hybrids.

or sow in the open ground about the end of April. This forms
a taller growing plant than the above, growing to 2–3 ft. The
flowers are a silvery-white with attractive inky reverse to the
ray petals, and are much prized for cutting (Pl. 87). Hybrids
with this species, known as *A. grandis* Hybrids, make vigorous
plants after the habit of *grandis*. The flower heads have long
stems valuable for cutting, with pale pastel shades of white,
ivory, buff, and salmon. A new group known as *Venidio-
Arctotis* Sutton's Triumph may be described here. The origin
of this group has been fully described in the R.H.S. Journal
1952, p. 361. The plants resemble those of Arctotis Special
Hybrids described above, but are more vigorous growing,
being very bushy in habit, the flower stems rising to 18 in.
to 2 ft, making the flowers useful for cutting (Pl. 88). The
colour range includes orange, yellow, golden-straw, salmon,
bronze, red, rich crimson, and wine. The plants are not quite

160

87. *Arctotis grandis.*

F

88. Venidio-Arctotis, Sutton's Triumph.

hardy, but may be planted out in mid-May, when they will come into flower and continue in full flower until October and November. They will not survive our winters and must be raised each year from cuttings taken in autumn and kept in a cool house or frost-proof frame during the winter.

Argemone: see Chapter 6 under Poppies.

Arnebia: Prophet Flower. From the Mediterranean region to the Himalayas; *Boraginaceae*.

A. cornuta comes from Afghanistan, and is an attractive H.H.A., useful for the mixed border and the rock garden, thriving in a well-drained soil and a sunny position. The dense flower spikes grow to 15–18 in., with deep green hairy foliage, the individual flowers being deep yellow with five vividly contrasting brownish-black spots.

Asperula: Woodruff; *Rubiaceae.*

A. orientalis (*A. azurea setosa*) is a H.A., native of Asia Minor. A slender growing branching plant 12 in., very useful for edgings and the front of the border. The small flowers are fragrant and lavender-blue in colour and when massed have a very beautiful effect. Also useful for cutting.

Aster, China: see Chapter 6.

Atriplex: Red Mountain Spinach; *Chenopodiaceae.*

A. hortensis rubra is an erect growing hardy annual growing to 4–5 ft. The crimson-coloured leaves and stems shot with violet make this a very useful subject for cutting for indoor decoration.

Auricula: see **Polyanthus.**

Baeria: California; *Compositae.*

B. coronaria (*Shortia californica*), a low-growing hardy annual from California, very useful for edgings and the front of the border, 6–9 in. with masses of golden-yellow daisy-like flowers, covering the attractive finely cut foliage.

Balsam: see **Impatiens.**

Bartonia: see **Mentzelia.**

Begonia: Tropical and Sub-Tropical Regions; *Begoniaceae.*

Two kinds of begonia are much used for bedding and also for pot work under glass, the tuberous rooted and fibrous rooted (Pl. 89). Both sorts are easily raised from seed. Sow under glass in a temperature of 65°F. in January and February in pots, well crocked to ensure good drainage and in a compost of equal parts of peat, light loam, and sand. The seed is exceedingly minute and must be sown thinly on the surface and simply pressed in. Prick out the tiny seedlings as soon as they can be handled into a similar compost and same temperature. They will grow quickly and can be potted on as soon as they can be handled and planted out in warm weather in June.

The tuberous rooted have a wide range of colours in both single and double forms including white, yellow, pink, scarlet, and crimson, and all these colours can be grown true from seed. They do best in rather a cool moist situation and will continue in flower the whole summer, making excellent pot plants for the cool greenhouse and for planting outdoors in June.

The fibrous rooted form compact bushy plants 9–15 in. high

89. Begonia, fibrous rooted.

and besides white are generally in shades of pink and red. On the Continent they are much used for bedding and will stand up to all kinds of weather, remaining in flower the whole summer. They also make very useful pot plants for the cool greenhouse.

Bellis: Daisy; Europe including the British Isles; *Compositae*.

Bellis perennis for garden purposes is best treated as a biennial. Sow seed in a cold frame or nursery bed, thinly, in very shallow drills in May or June, prick out in the open, and plant in flowering position in autumn. The large double-flowered strains make excellent plants for spring bedding, either by themselves or as groundwork for bulbs and other taller growing subjects. The petals may be flat or quilled. The flat may be obtained in giant white, pink, and crimson, the quilled in salmon-pink – a very beautiful shade without the 'beetroot' tint – and bright crimson. These all grow 9–12 in. A miniature double-flowered strain is now offered with very free-flowering plants only 6 in. These all make charming pot plants for the cold house and are also delightful as cut flowers in low bowls.

Bidens atrosanguinea: see **Cosmos diversifolius atrosanguineus.**

Brachycome iberidifolia: see **Swan River Daisy.**

Browallia: South America; *Solanaceae.*

Browallia speciosa major, although a tender perennial, makes a useful pot plant for the cool greenhouse, flowering in late summer and autumn from a spring sowing. 18 in. to 2 ft with large bright blue flowers. They are of easy cultivation and flower over a long period. From a sowing made in July and August plants may be brought into flower in the greenhouse during winter and early spring.

Another species, *B. demissa* (*elata*), will flower outside in a warm situation and may also be grown as pot plants in the cool greenhouse, 1–1½ ft, with smaller flowers than the above, soft violet-blue.

Cacalia coccinea: see *Emilia flammea.*

Calandrinia: Rock Purslane; America and Australia; *Portula-caceae.*

Useful garden plants, the most widely grown being *C. umbellata* from Peru, a compact bushy plant 6 in. with narrow dark green leaves and vivid crimson-magenta flowers, which close at night. This can be treated as a H.H.A. and planted out in a warm, well-drained sandy soil where, unless the winters are too severe, it will persist for two or three years. The colour of the flowers is one of the most intense in the garden and in sunshine is positively dazzling. For this reason the plant must be placed with care. Other species which may be grown as H.H.A. are *C. grandiflora* from Chile, 12–18 in. with fleshy leaves and rose-coloured flowers and *C. menziesii* (*speciosa*), California 6–9 in. with ruby coloured flowers.

Calceolaria: Slipperwort; Central and South America; *Scrophu-lariaceae.*

The genus *Calceolaria* contains several annual and perennial species and for garden purposes may be divided into shrubby and herbaceous kinds.

165

90. Calceolaria 'Sutton's Perfection'

The herbaceous calceolarias, sometimes known as $C. \times$ *herbeohybrida* probably originated from a hybrid between *C. corymbosa* and *C. crenatiflora*. They make showy cool greenhouse plants 15–18 in. and as much across, with handsome deep green foliage which well sets off the large trusses of vivid coloured flowers. Very varied in colour including bright shades of orange, yellow, and red, besides the softer apricots, rose, and terra-cotta.

A useful dwarfer-growing group, C. multiflora nana or Dwarf mixed has similar coloured flowers but grows 9–12 in. with trusses of smaller sized flowers, making it more suited to the smaller greenhouse and market work.

As calceolaria species hybridize easily, other hybrid groups have been produced and are well worthy of a place in the cool greenhouse. $C. \times profusa$ (*clibranii*) grows 2–3 ft with tall graceful sprays of rich golden-yellow medium-sized flowers. *C.* × *gracilis* (John Innes Strain) carries sprays of small dainty flowers 18 in. to 2 ft with a charming range of delicate colouring varying from creamy-pink to mauve.

The greenhouse calceolaria should be sown in June and July for flowering the following spring and early summer. Sow in cool shady conditions and winter in cold frames from which frost can be excluded. The plants should be kept cool at all times and brought into the greenhouse just before coming into flower.

C. mexicana, 12 in., is a hardy annual species from Mexico, which can be sown in the open ground, with soft pale yellow flowers about the size of a sixpence and carried in heads well above the deep green, finely cut foliage. This will stand shade and is attractive for informal drifts in the woodland garden.

Calendula: see Chapter 6 under Pot Marigold.

Calliopsis: see **Coreopsis.**

Callistephus chinensis: see Chapter 6 under China Aster.

Campanula: *Campanulaceae.*

C. medium. Canterbury bell. This well known showy biennial is of South European origin and has been in our gardens for over 300 years. It is an easily grown garden plant. Sow May and June, and plant out in flowering position in early autumn. Guard against slugs in the seedling stage. The flowers are produced at a useful time of the year, namely in May and June, the large spikes rising to a height of 2–3 ft in a well-grown plant. Colours include white, shades of pink, blue, and mauve, and come true from seed. There are true singles, double-flowered forms, and *calycanthema* or cup and saucer (Pl.91). Canterbury bells are useful in clumps in the mixed border, and in the woodland garden. They may also be potted up in autumn for flowering in the cold greenhouse in spring and early summer.

An annual form is available which if sown in gentle heat in spring, will flower in July and August.

Campanula persicifolia (the Peach-leaved campanula), also from Europe, although a perennial, may also be easily raised from seed and treated as a biennial, similar to the Canterbury bell. This makes a beautiful plant with tall slender spikes 2–3 ft of

167

91. Canterbury Bell, cup and saucer variety.

bell-like flowers in pure white, pale blue, and dark blue, coming true from seed. Delightful for cutting. *C. carpatica* is another perennial species which can be similarly treated and easily and economically raised from seed. This is a dwarf-growing plant 6–12 in. Plant in full sun where it is excellent for the rock garden and edgings. Colours coming true from seed include white, pale blue, and dark blue. A low-growing dwarfer strain known as 'Gem' will come true from seed in similar colours.

Campanula specularia: see **Venus's Looking-Glass.**

Canary Creeper: see Chapter 6 under Nasturtium.

Candytuft: see **Iberis.**

Celosia argentea (*C. plumosa*): Cockscomb; Tropical Asia; *Amaranthaceae.*

Celosias require moisture and heat and are best grown under glass in this country although in certain warm sheltered

92. *Celosia argentea* (*plumosa*).

gardens they may be used for summer bedding where they make an unusual effect.

The feathered forms are on the whole to be preferred to the 'crested' or true cockscomb type although the latter have been used effectively for decoration purposes. Sow in March in heat and keep growing on without a check, finally potting singly into 6-in. pots in a rich compost. Well-grown plants are very decorative in pots under glass, making large spikes 15–18 in. in crimson and scarlet and a rich honey-coloured yellow. The cockscomb type is offered in a mixture which includes white, gold, orange, rose, and rich crimson shades. It is important to get a good strain.

Celsia: Mediterranean and eastwards to India. *Scrophulariaceae.*
C. arcturus. A good flowering pot plant for the cool greenhouse with large spikes of clear yellow flowers with purple anthers. 18 in. to 2 ft. From seed sown in gentle heat in February it will flower in six months and remain in flower for at least two months. H.H.P.

C. cretica. A hardy biennial in favoured situations making a good border plant and useful in pots in the cool greenhouse. Frequently treated as H.H.A. Sow in heat in March for autumn flowering outside and in August for winter and spring flowering under glass. Tall spikes, 5–6 ft, of large sweetly-scented golden-yellow flowers quaintly marked by two brown spots.

Centaurea cyanus: see Chapter 6 under Cornflower.

Centaurea moschata (Sweet Sultan) from the Eastern Mediterranean has long been known in gardens and is well worth growing (Pl. 93). The strain known as Imperialis or Giant – said to be of hybrid origin, is the best, branching 3 ft or more. The fragrant flower heads have long stems and are very useful for cutting. Colours include pure white, delicate mauve, deep mauve, and purple, also yellow, the blooms of which are some-what smaller. The flower heads should be cut young, when they last longer in water. Sow in the open ground in April to flower all summer, or in favourable situations in September, when they will make extra strong-growing plants which flower earlier. They flourish in a well-cultivated soil with sufficient lime in open sunny situations.

93. *Centaurea moschata* (Sweet Sultan).

Charieis heterophylla: S. Africa; *Compositae.*

A dwarf-growing annual with rich blue daisy-like flowers. Sow in open ground in April in a sunny situation. Height 6 in. Sometimes listed as *Kaulfussia amelloides.*

Cheiranthus: see Chapter 6 under Wallflower.

Cheiranthus allionii: see Chapter 6 under Wallflower, Siberian.

Chrysanthemum: annual; see Chapter 6.

Chrysanthemum parthenium: see **Matricaria.**

Cineraria: Canary Islands; *Compositae.*

The garden cineraria has been derived from *Senecio cruentus* and makes one of the most useful plants for the spring and early summer decoration of the cool greenhouse. Seed should be sown in May and June and the plants grown quite cool throughout, only giving sufficient heat to keep out frost. Shade from hot sun. The principal groups are:

Large flowered single. Plants of compact habit 1–2 ft high. Large flower heads with a wide range of colouring including white, pink, rose-purple, blue, and scarlet, usually offered in mixture.

Intermediate. A similar strain to the large flowered single but with smaller flowers and more compact heads. Offered in mixture and several colours separately, including scarlet and blue.

Stellata or Star. Taller than above and with wide spreading corymbs of small star-like flowers in a wide range of colouring, mostly pink and blue shades and frequently offered separately. 2–3 ft.

Feltham Beauty Strain. Similar to above but more compact, flowers in a mixture of shades with white centres.

Multiflora nana or dwarf. Dwarf compact group, very showy and with a rich range of colouring in mixture. 1 ft.

Cineraria: annual; see *Senecio arenarius.*

Cladanthus arabicus: Mediterranean; *Compositae.*

An interesting H.A. with bright yellow daisy-like flowers and fern-like foliage. 15–18 in. Likes full sun. Often grown under name *Anthemis arabica.*

Clarkia: California; *Onagraceae.*

C. elegans (Pl.94) is one of the many useful H.A. which have

94. *Clarkia elegans* 'Brilliant Mixture'.

come out of California. This is the species from which most of the clarkias grown in gardens today have arisen. Sow in place both in spring and in favourable positions in autumn. Those from the latter sowing make handsome plants 2–3 ft while from the former the plants are 12–18 in. The habit of a well-grown plant is branching and pyramidal with long spikes of flowers, the buds opening in water which makes them very useful for cutting. By selection the colour range has been greatly widened and the flowers increased in size and number of petals. Colours include pure white, pale pink, salmon-pink, salmon-scarlet, bright rose, and deep purple, all offered from seed separately and in mixture.

The culture is easy but they do respond to well-cultivated soil, an open sunny situation, and early staking. They make excellent pot plants for the cool house; sow either in September or October to flower May and June, or in spring to flower June and July.

Cleome: Spider Plant; Southern States of America; *Capparidaceae*.

C. spinosa (Pl. 95) is a handsome H.H.A., 3–4 ft. The stems end in a large cluster of four-petalled flowers bearing long prominent stamens giving a spidery look to the flower, hence its name. The whole plant and leaves are covered with sharp spines and when bruised the leaves have rather an unpleasant smell. In spite of these drawbacks cleomes are well worth growing for their handsome habit and decorative appearance. The type has light purple flowers. There is an excellent pink, 'Pink Queen', and a good white. The plants remain in flower for several months during the summer. Sow in March in gentle heat and plant out in May in a warm, well-cultivated soil, and do not allow to become too dry.

Cobaea: Mexico; *Polemoniaceae*.

C. scandens is a most useful vigorous growing climber, which, although a half-hardy perennial, may conveniently be grown as a H.H.A. The plants will rapidly cover walls, trellis-work, a porch, or similar positions. The flowers are bell-shaped and borne on long stems, green and violet, and are much used for decorative work owing to their unusual and attractive

174

95. *Cleome spinosa* (the Spider plant).

colouring. July–October. Can also be grown in a greenhouse when there is room. The flat seeds should be sown edge downwards in March. Prick out into small pots and plant out in a sunny, sheltered position in June.

Coleus: Tropics; *Labiatae.*

From the species *C. blumei* have arisen the beautiful foliage plants with attractive coloured leaves and quaint markings, much used as pot plants in greenhouses and for window boxes. Various names are used to denote strains having a wide range of coloured foliage, such as 'Prize', 'Monarch', and 'Giant'. Easily raised from seed sown in gentle heat in February and March.

C. frederici. A good winter flowering plant 3–4 ft for the cool greenhouse, with long spikes of light blue fragrant flowers in December. Sow in February or March and pot on as required.

Collinsia bicolor: California; *Scrophulariaceae.*

An easily grown and beautiful H.A. forming slender plants

12–15 in. and from a spring sowing giving long spikes of lilac and white flowers lasting over several weeks. Can also be sown in place in autumn in favourable situations. Attractive as pot plants and as they will stand light shade may be grown in drifts in the woodland garden. A desirable garden annual.

Collomia biflora (*coccinea*): Chile; *Polemoniaceae*.

An attractive H.A. which may be sown in spring or autumn 15–18 in., the stems terminating in clusters of small gilia-like flowers, cherry-red, favoured by bees. Open sunny situation.

Convolvulus: see **Ipomoea** for Morning Glory.

Convolvulus: Southern Europe; *Convolvulaceae*.

C. tricolor (*minor*) (Pl. 96). The dwarf convolvulus of gardens is a bright showy H.A. The bushy plants grow 12–15 in. and when in full sun make a brilliant show in flower. The large funnel-shaped flowers can be obtained true from seed in pale blue, dark blue, rose, and pink.

C. major (*Ipomoea purpurea*). The climbing convolvulus. This useful climber although not very hardy may be sown in the open in early May. It is a rapid grower and will quickly cover a fence or trellis-work or grow over and through a hedge. There is a wide range of colouring including blue, pale blue, carmine, purple, rose, and white, many of which come true from seed. July–September.

Coreopsis: Tick-seed; North America; *Compositae*

The forms of *C. tinctoria* are many and variable, both in colour and habit of growth. The colour is mainly yellow and crimson-brown and the height varies from 9 to 12 in. up to 2–3 ft and more. The dwarfer forms are useful for groups in the mixed border, for pot plants, and for bedding and are brilliant in sunshine. The taller forms are very graceful in habit and useful as cut flowers, giving colour in the garden in late summer and autumn. 'Atrosanguinea' (Pl. 97) is a fine form with rich dark red flowers; 'Marmorata' has the flowers curiously marbled and striped. The flowers of the type itself are yellow and brown. These taller forms should be carefully supported by twiggy stakes and room should always be found for them in the cutting garden.

C. drummondii. One of the best species with large clear

96. *Convolvulus tricolor* 'Royal Ensign'.

97. *Coreopsis tinctoria* 'Atrosanguinea'.

98. Coreopsis, annual dwarf variety.

yellow flowers, 1½–2 ft. All are H.A. and should be sown in April where they are to flower.

C. maritima and *C. stillmanni:* see **Leptosyne.**

Cornflower: see Chapter 6.

Cosmos: Cosmea; Mexico; *Compositae.*

The early-flowering strain of *C. bipinnatus* sown in March under glass and planted out in May is worthy of a place in every garden, 3–4 ft, flowering right through the summer until autumn. With their finely cut fresh green foliage and vigorous branching habit, cosmeas make a useful addition to the mixed border, the annual border, and the cutting garden. The large single flowers are borne on long wiry stems; colours include pure white, pink, rose-pink, crimson, and a later addition, crimson-scarlet. A recent introduction from America, called 'Pink Sensation', has large rich pink flowers with a crimson zone in the centre.

C. sulphureus bears golden-yellow flowers, the best variety for

179

99. *Cosmos sulphureus* 'Orange Ruffles'.

this country being 'Orange Ruffles' (Pl. 99), with semi-double, glowing-orange flowers, 18 in., flowering soon after planting out in May from a March sowing under glass. The plants are much more slender in growth and the flowers smaller than those of *C. bipinnatus*, but are worth growing for their colour alone. H.H.A.

C. diversifolius atrosanguineus (*Bidens atrosanguinea*), Black Cosmos. A plant with a certain charm, bearing dark velvety-red flowers resembling a small single dahlia, with finely cut foliage and slender stems 15–18 in. A tender perennial which succeeds well as a H.H.A. in a warm sunny situation, July–October.

Cotula: The Pin-cushion Plant; S. Africa; *Compositae*.

C. barbata (*Cenia barbata*). A neat tufted little plant with narrow silky hairy leaves from which arise on long stalks rayless heads of pale yellow flowers (Pl. 100). 9 in. Delightful for the rock garden, in pots in the cool greenhouse, and for edgings. Sow under glass in March and plant out in May. H.H.A.

Cuphea: Cigar Plant; Mexico; *Lythraceae*.

C. ignea (*C. platycentra*). Showy bedding or pot plant of dwarf bushy habit, 12 in. Easily raised from seed sown in heat in February and potted on in rich soil. Useful pot plants for the greenhouse flowering over a long period. The unusual

100. *Cotula barbata*
     (the pin-cushion
     plant).

shaped flowers consist of a narrow scarlet tube, with a dark ring at the base and a white mouth. For bedding, plant in a warm sheltered situation. H.H.A.

C. miniata, 9–12 in. Bright red flowers. Flowers July–September. H.H.A.

Cynoglossum amabile: Hound's Tongue; China; *Boraginaceae*.

A charming hardy biennial which will flower the same year if sown in March under glass and planted out in May. Seed may also be sown in the open ground in April where the plants will flower in late summer. 1–2 ft; the turquoise-blue flowers are attractively set off by the grey-green downy foliage.

Dahlia hybrida: Central America; *Compositae*.

The modern dahlia is of complex hybrid origin and during the last twenty or thirty years many separate types have been developed showing a very wide variation in habit of plant, size, and colouring of flower.

For ordinary garden purposes dahlias are increasingly propagated from seed, and thus treated as a H.H.A. The most satisfactory for this purpose are the dwarfer growing sections.

The dwarf-growing single flowered or Coltness group forms plants 12–18 in. high and as much across; it is offered in good mixtures and also in separate colours, white, yellow, pink shades, scarlet, and crimson, all coming true from seed. In order to prolong flowering, it is important to remove the flower heads as they fade.

Dwarf-growing groups with small decorative double or semi-double flower heads (Pl. 101) are also very satisfactory from seed, such as Unwin's Dwarf Hybrids growing 1½–2 ft, and 'Sutton's Dwarf Border' in a very wide range of colour and forming very free-flowering plants 2–2½ ft high. The double and semi-double flowers are borne well above the foliage and beside being useful for the mixed border, are also delightful as cut flowers. The beauty of this group is that owing to their bushy compact habit the plants require no staking. They come true in several colours from seed, including pure white, soft yellow, pink shades, and red shades.

The tall giant doubles are not so satisfactory from seed but the Tall Giant Single gives a wide range of colouring, the

101. Dahlia, Sutton's Dwarf Border.

plants growing to a height of 5–6 ft with large single flowers. They must be securely staked and are admirable for the back of the mixed border.

Their wide diversity of forms, the vividness and wide range of colouring of their flowers, and the ease of their cultivation make the modern dahlia unsurpassed for decoration in the garden in beds and borders and also for use as cut flowers. With regard to cultivation from seed, one of the main points to remember, and, contrary to the too common recommendation, is not to sow the seed too early. Seed should not be sown before the end of March or even in early April. Raise in gentle heat and prick off singly into 3-in. pots as soon as they are large enough to handle, potting on into 5-in. ones, and finally planting out into flowering positions when all danger from frost is over. The dahlia is a plant which responds to a good rich soil, must not lack for moisture, and likes full sun.

Daisy: see **Bellis**.

Datura: Angel's Trumpets; Mexico; *Solanaceae*.

The daturas are not seen in gardens today as much as they were. They make striking plants in the flower border with their handsome trumpet-shaped flowers and attractive leaves. In many cases the flowers are also sweetly scented. They do best in the southern parts of the country in warm sunny situations. Treat as H.H.A., sow in heat in April and plant out at end of May and early June. They also make very attractive pot plants flowering over a long period in the cool greenhouse.

D. metel var. *chlorantha*. 3–4 ft, long pendulous golden-yellow flowers.

D. metel var. *fastuosa* (*D. cornucopia*). 2–3 ft, flowers white tinged with purple, sweetly scented.

D. meteloides. A very handsome species with luxuriant foliage and white, sweetly scented flowers suffused with purple. 3–4 ft.

Delphinium hybridum: Garden origin; *Ranunculaceae*.

For Larkspur (*D. ajacis* and *D. consolida*) or Annual Delphinium see Chapter 6.

The modern perennial delphinium, which arose from crosses with *D. elatum* and other species is so often nowadays raised from seed and treated as a biennial or even an annual that a short note may be useful.

The two main types of perennial delphinium grown in gardens are:

D. hybridum, which includes the tall robust border plants, 5–6 ft. Several colours now come true from seed including pure white, deep bright blue, and sky blue. A new group of this type called 'Pacific' has come from America, with a wide range of beautiful colours and spikes of very large open florets. *D. belladonna*, also easily raised from seed, forms a dwarfer-growing branching plant 3 ft high with loose spikes of flowers, useful for cutting, flowering slightly earlier than the *hybridum* types.

102. *Delphinium hybridum* 'Sutton's White'.

Two colours, pale blue and dark blue, come perfectly true from seed.

The best method of raising from seed is to sow the seed in February or March in gentle heat, prick out the seedlings into sheltered nursery beds, in lines say 9 in. by 6 in. and the resulting plants will flower in August and September of the same year throwing handsome spikes 3–4 ft long. Guard the young seedlings against slugs.

The following spring the plants, as they show signs of growth, may be conveniently planted into their permanent flowering positions. Slugs are very destructive to the young shoots just as they are showing growth. A simple preventative is to cover the crown completely with several inches of cinders.

D. paniculatum. A hardy annual species from the Balkans. Very free-branching plants 18 in. to 2 ft, with wiry stems and finely cut foliage, bearing tiny violet-blue flowers.

D. grandiflorum. The Chinese delphinium. The Chinese delphinium *D. grandiflorum* (Pl. 103), sometimes called *D. chinense*, although a perennial, is best treated in most gardens as a H.H.A. Unlike the larkspurs this transplants easily and may be raised by sowing in early March in gentle heat, pricking out into boxes, and planting out in May to form bushy free-flowering plants 12 in. high and as much across, flowering in July and August. Seed may also be sown in August and the resulting seedlings pricked out into small pots and wintered in cold frames. Plant out in spring when the plants will flower from June onwards. Varieties having bright blue, pale blue, and white flowers are offered. One of the best is 'Blue Butterfly'. A recent variety is 'Dwarf Gentian Blue', which is useful in the rock garden, as edgings, in windows boxes, or for pot work.

Dianthus: Annual Carnation; *Caryophyllaceae.*

D. caryophyllus – the annual carnation is a native of southern France where it is widely grown and has been much developed as a decorative garden plant (Pl. 104). Really biennial, it succeeds so well as a H.H.A. that it is usually treated in this way. The varieties include a very wide range of colours coming practically true from seed, including pure white, yellow,

186

103. *Delphinium grandiflorum*, dwarf variety.

salmon, rose-pink, scarlet, and crimson. The plants come into full flower in August and September, giving an abundance of flowers on stems of 15–18 in. When frost approaches, the plants may be lifted, carefully potted, and brought into the cool greenhouse to provide flowers during the winter. Sow the seed under glass in January or February, keep the seedlings cool with abundant light and air, and plant out in May in an open sunny well-drained position.

D. barbatus – Annual sweet william (Pl. 105). This strain has been much improved recently and now provides a full range of sweet william colouring and marking in bushy free-flowering plants 15–18 in., coming into full flower in July and August from a sowing under glass in early March.

187

104. Annual carnation, Improved Marguerite.

105. Annual Sweet William 'Sutton's Summer Beauty'.

A hybrid known as *Dianthus* Sweet Wivelsfield gives a brilliant mixture of colours. Treatment similar to the above.

D. chinensis (*D. sinensis*), Chinese, Japanese, or Indian Pink, a native of E. Asia. The most widely grown is the group Heddewigii – the Japanese Pink, grown in the nineteenth century by Carl Heddewig, a gardener of St Petersburg, from seed imported from Japan, and probably taken from long cultivated oriental garden forms. The present day varieties have a compact free-flowering habit and showy flowers with a wide range of colour (Pl. 106). Some of them have the petals beautifully fringed and exquisitely marked.

189

106. *Dianthus chinensis* (Heddewigii) 'Brilliant Fringed'.

Varieties may be grown with single and double flowers; the colours in the singles include a good pure white, pink, scarlet, crimson, and a delightful mixture known as Brilliant Fringed Mixed. The doubles include also pure white, delicate pink, rich pink, scarlet, crimson, and violet, and an interesting variety 'Black Prince' with maroon black petals charmingly edged with silvery white, and 'Diadem' which has pink, rose, crimson, and purple grounds, marked with black. Useful for bedding, for the mixed border, for cut flowers, and for pot plants for the cool greenhouse. They prefer a good loamy soil in full sunshine, but, like the annual phloxes, like moisture and cool conditions when young. Sow early March and plant out as early as is safe in May. Watch for thrips in the early stages; even a preventive spray in the boxes before planting out is well worth while. In fact for all half-hardy annuals, a good routine rule is always to spray the boxes with a simple insecticide just before planting out.

Didiscus caeruleus: see Trachymene.

Digitalis: see Chapter 6 under Foxglove.

Dimorphotheca: see Chapter 6.

Dorotheanthus bellidiflorus: see **Mesembryanthemum.**

Eccremocarpus: Chile; *Bignoniaceae.*

E. scaber. This attractive Chilean climber, although a perennial and persistent only in well-sheltered places in mild winters, is capable of flowering well in many gardens in this country as a H.H.A. Height 8–10 ft, with clusters of orange-scarlet flowers the whole summer. Sow under glass in March and plant out when all risk of frost is over in full sun.

Echinops: Globe Thistle; *Compositae.*

E. ritro. An easily grown hardy perennial useful for the mixed border, the semi-wild garden, and for cutting. Rather a coarse thistle-like plant producing rich blue globular heads of flowers on long stems 3 ft high. Easily flowered as a hardy biennial by being sown in nursery lines in the open ground in May and June and planted into flowering position in autumn.

107. *Echium plantagineum*, dwarf hybrids.

191

Echium: Vipers Bugloss; chiefly Mediterranean Region; *Boraginaceae*.

E. plantagineum (Pl. 107) – an annual which has been very much improved from a garden point of view in recent years. This plant and its modern varieties deserve to be much more widely grown. It can be sown in place as a hardy annual, or be transplanted. Originally the type was a strong-growing, free-flowering plant 18 in. to 2 ft, bearing violet-blue flowers; a bright blue was first selected and bred true, then a rose-pink and pure white. Now compact bushy forms are available from seed, 9–12 in. in height and with a wide range of soft pastel shades of blue, mauve, purple, rose-pink, and white. The individual flowers have also at the same time been enlarged, the result being a charming mixture for the mixed border, the rock garden, and for edgings. This plant has the added usefulness of succeeding under very variable conditions, in cold, wet, and windy seasons and equally well in the very opposite, dry and sunny. The taller varieties are also useful for drifts in the semi-wild garden.

Emilia: Tassel Flower; Tropical America; *Compositae*.

E. flammea (*Cacalia coccinea*). A charming easily grown hardy annual. The flowers are orange-scarlet in colour and resemble miniature tassels. They are borne in clusters on long wiry stems about 18 in. high. Very graceful as cut flowers. Grow in a warm sunny position in a well-drained light soil.

Erinus: Western Europe; *Scrophulariaceae*.

E. alpinus, a native of the mountains naturalized in certain parts of Great Britain. This forms a tufted alpine plant with deeply toothed small dark green leaves from which arise clusters of small purple flowers borne on stems 5–6 in. Sow in gritty soil in March in pans or even in the crevices of brick walls where the plants will soon establish themselves. From a spring sowing the plants will flower the following March–June. There is a pink-flowered form which comes true from seed, the colour being much preferred to the type. A white variety is also available.

Eryngium: Sea Holly; *Umbelliferae*.

Decorative hardy perennials easily treated as biennials and well worth growing for decorative purposes both in the garden and for cutting.

E. amethystinum. 1–2 ft. Flowers July–August. Flower heads amethyst.

E. giganteum. Silver Thistle. 3–4 ft. Spiny leaves with silvery metallic surface. Flower heads blue.

E. planum. 2 ft. Blue stems and foliage.

Erysimum allionii: see Chapter 6 under Wallflower, Siberian.

Eschscholzia: see Chapter 6.

Euphorbia: Spurge; Southern States of America; *Euphorbiaceae.*

E. heterophylla, sometimes known as the annual poinsettia or Mexican Fire Plant, is a H.A., about 2 ft. The small orange-red flowers are borne in clusters at the ends of the stems and the surrounding leaves become attractively coloured, being marked with bright red at the base or blotched with red and white from July to September. The seeds may also be sown in gentle heat in March giving the plants more time to develop. The bushy plants make excellent pot plants. The unusual colouring and the attractively shaped leaves are very useful for decoration.

E. marginata, Snow on the Mountain. A strikingly decorative plant with light green leaves veined and margined with white. Very decorative for cutting. Can be treated as a H.A. sown in place in April or sown earlier under glass in March and planted out in May, 12 in. apart. Height 2 ft.

Evening Primrose: see **Oenothera.**

Exacum: South Indian Ocean region; *Gentianaceae.*

E. affine, a warm greenhouse annual from the Island of Socotra. From a sowing in March in a well-drained peaty soil in 60–65° F. well-grown plants may be obtained in flower in late summer and autumn. They require warm conditions when young but as they come into flower may be placed in the cool greenhouse. Bushy branching plants, 12–15 in. with small shiny green foliage. From the axis of each leaf small violet-blue flowers are produced with prominent yellow stamens. They are deliciously scented and the plants remain in flower for several months. To get larger earlier-flowering plants, provided sufficient heat can be maintained, seed may also be sown in August and September.

Felicia: South Africa; *Compositae*.

The felicias include annual and perennial species and provide us with some very useful garden plants.

F. affinis, an easily grown H.H.A. with deep blue daisy-like flowers and rich yellow centres, borne on long stalks well above the foliage. 6–9 in. Makes a useful pot plant for the cool house and for patches in the border. Sow under glass in mid-March.

F. amelloides (*Agathaea coelestis*), a half-hardy perennial species easily flowered as a H.H.A. and often grown as a greenhouse perennial. From a sowing in spring, bushy plants can be produced which will provide a mass of pale blue flowers from July to October. The plants can then be lifted, potted, and brought under glass to continue flowering during the winter, or better still another sowing can be made in June–July to provide plants in pots for the cool greenhouse which will flower from Christmas onwards.

F. bergeriana – Kingfisher Daisy (Pl. 108) – a small dwarf-growing H.H.A. which will flower most of the summer through, in a warm sunny situation, the flower stems rising 4–5 in. above the foliage, the small flower heads being bright metallic blue in colour. Apt to close in dull weather. Very useful for the rock garden and for front positions in the annual border.

Foxglove: see Chapter 6.

Gaillardia: Blanket-Flower; America; *Compositae*.

Annual gaillardias should be sown under glass in March and planted out in May. They will then begin to flower in July and continue in flower until autumn. They form bushy free-flowering plants 15–18 in. and the flowers are very useful for cutting. *G. pulchella* is the species from which most of the garden varieties have been derived. The crimson-purple flowers are tipped with yellow and double-flowered forms are also available. A variety with coppery-scarlet flowers is also offered.

Gazania: South Africa; *Compositae*.

By hybridization and selection gazanias have been much improved for garden purposes in recent years. The species, as is often the case in the *Compositae*, hybridize freely and the new

108. *Felicia bergeriana* 'Azure Blue'.

hybrids can be grown very easily as H.H.A. Sow seed in gentle heat in February, and plant out as early as possible in May. Gazanias will even stand a slight ground frost and it is a help to plant out as early as possible.

The plants will begin to flower in June and continue into the autumn, in an open sunny situation. Planted at 12 in. apart each way, they will cover the ground and, especially if the withered flower heads are removed, will flower for several months. The size of flower and colouring have been greatly improved and two mixtures of colours are now available true from seed – Red and Orange Shades, and Pink and Cream Shades. The ray petals are very beautifully marked with contrasting zones of unusual colouring and in many cases conspicuously spotted. The flower heads open in sunshine only and close by three o'clock in the afternoon (Pl. 109).

Gilia: California; *Polemoniaceae*.

The species of gilia come mainly from North America and a few from the Andes in South America. Only a few of the most widely grown of the annual species are mentioned here and one biennial. They all prefer a light well-drained soil in full sun.

G. capitata – an erect-growing branching H.A. with heads of soft lavender-blue flowers carried well above the finely cut foliage. 1½–2 ft.

G. × hybrida (*Leptosiphon hybridus*) – a diffusely branched hardy annual with finely-cut leaves and bearing dense heads of tiny flowers in a wide range of colouring, in yellow, orange, red, rose, purple, and violet. Very useful in the rock garden, in flagged paths, and in clumps in the front of the annual border. 3–6 in.

G. rubra (*G. coronopifolia*). The Scarlet Gilia. A striking biennial growing to a height of 3–4 or more feet. Tall usually single stems clothed all the way up with finely cut foliage and terminating in many plumed spikes of brilliant scarlet flowers. Best sown in September under glass, potted singly into small pots and kept in the cool greenhouse until spring when the plants may be put out in the mixed border. Flowers July–October. Seed sown in heat in the early spring will flower the same year in autumn.

196

109. Gazania hybrids.

Colour variations in pink, yellow, and orange also occur.

G. tricolor (*G. nivalis*) – a diffuse slender growing H.A., 12–18 in. with dense heads of small flowers in various shades of colour including pure white, lavender, and white with golden and purple centres, also pink. Useful for massing in clumps in the annual border.

Glaucium: Horned Poppy; see Chapter 6 under Poppies.

Godetia: see Chapter 6.

Grasses, Ornamental.

Many grass species are very ornamental when in flower, and can be easily raised from seed sown in the place where they are to flower. They are useful for decorative patches in the mixed border, make excellent pot plants, and are indispensable in the cutting garden. Many can also be cut and carefully dried for use in winter decoration (Pl. 19). Here are a few of the most useful and easily grown.

Agrostis nebulosa, Cloud Grass. H.A.

Agrostis laxiflora. H.A.

Agrostis pulchella (*Aira capillaris* var. *pulchella*), Hair Grass. H.A.

Anthoxanthum gracilis, a dwarf ornamental grass useful for edgings. H.A.

Avena sterilis, Animated Oat. H.A.

Briza maxima, Quaking Grass. H.A.

Briza minor. H.A.

Bromus briziformis. H.A.

Coix lacryma-jobi. H.H.A. Job's Tears.

Eragrostis, Love Grass. H.A.

Three species are all worth growing – *E. maxima*, *E. abyssinica*, and *E. elegans*.

Hordeum jubatum, Squirrel-tail Grass. H.A.

Lagurus ovatus, Hare's Tail Grass. H.A.

Stipa pennata, Feather Grass – a beautiful grass with 20 in. stems. H.P.

Gypsophila: *Caryophyllaceae*.

G. elegans, a slender, grey-leaved H.A., 12–18 in., bearing clusters of small white flowers, much used for decoration. A larger flowered strain, well known in Covent Garden Market, is also offered and a pink flowered form. *G. viscosa*, a native of Syria and southern Asia Minor, is sometimes offered as *G. elegans*, crimson. A very attractive variety bearing rich crimson flowers on slender dark stems. H.A.

Helianthus: see Chapter 6 under Sunflower.

Helichrysum: Everlasting; Australia; *Compositae*.

H. bracteatum, well-known H.H.A., native of Australia.

The flowers show a wide range of colouring, including silvery white, rich yellow, salmon-pink, rich red, and crimson, many of the colours coming true from seed. The dried flowers are much used for winter decoration (Pl. 110). For this purpose they should be grown in the cutting garden, the flowers being picked just as they open and before the yellow centres are showing. Cut and hang in bunches in a cool airy place. A

110. Helichrysum, double mixed.

dwarf form is also offered in a wide range of colouring, with bushy plants 12–15 in. From a sowing under glass in March and planted out in May, strong growing plants may be obtained making a height of 2–3 ft. It may be sown in warm sunny positions in open ground in April and May.

Heliotropium: Heliotrope or Cherry Pie; Peru; *Boraginaceae*.

H. corymbosum and *H. peruvianum* are the progenitors of the modern garden strains of Heliotrope or Cherry Pie. Although strictly speaking a greenhouse perennial, varieties may now be obtained which flower freely in a few months from seed. These modern varieties form compact branching plants 12–18 in., bearing large trusses of flowers carried well above the foliage. Sow in February and early March in gentle heat and pot on the seedlings into small pots planting out towards the end of May. The early flowering strains produce sweetly scented flowers from early July onwards and are very useful for the front of a sunny border, underneath a south window, and so on. The plants may also be potted up for growing on in the cool greenhouse. The colours available include pure white, all shades of blue and heliotrope to purple and crimson, many coming remarkably true from seed.

Helipterum: Australia; *Compositae.*

This group of everlasting flowers now includes *Acroclinium* and *Rhodanthe*.

H. manglesii, sometimes offered as *Rhodanthe*, forms a bushy, free-flowering plant, 12–15 in. high, with nodding globular heads of flowers in pink and white. Can be raised under glass in March or sown in the open in a warm sunny situation in April. It also makes an attractive pot plant for the cool greenhouse, putting 4 or 5 seedlings in a 5-in. pot. The flower heads can be dried and preserved for winter decoration like the helichrysum.

H. roseum, sometimes offered as *Acroclinium*, is a delightful hardy annual, and easily grown in full sun (Pl. 111). Sow in place in April. 15–18 in., the narrow leaves being somewhat succulent and a glaucous green. The stems terminate in daisy-like flower heads, pure white, pink, and shades of rose with attractive golden yellow and dark coloured centres. Some of the shades of deep pink with dark centres are very attractive. As

111. *Helipterum (Acroclinium) roseum.*

H

the flowers are produced on long single stems, they are particularly useful for cutting. Can also be grown in pots similarly to *Rhodanthe*. Used also for winter decoration.

Heracleum: Giant Parsnip; Caucasus; *Umbelliferae.*

H. villosum. A stately plant for the wild garden, 10–12 ft, suitable for growing in light woodland and in moist soil. The plant bears handsome foliage and immense flat umbels of flowers. Treat as a hardy biennial.

Hesperis matronalis: see **Sweet Rocket.**

Hollyhock: see **Althaea.**

Honesty: see **Lunaria.**

Humulus: Hop; China and Japan; *Urticaceae.*

H. japonicus (*H. scandens*), truly a perennial but easily grown as an annual.

Sow under glass in March planting out in May or can be sown in the open ground in May. A vigorous climber with light green foliage quickly covering trellis-work, arbours, and fences. The plants grow quite well in towns. A variegated form is available.

Hunnemannia fumariifolia: see Chapter 6 under Poppies.

Iberis: Candytuft; Europe including southern Britain; *Cruciferae.* A popular dwarf-growing H.A. The common candytuft, *I. umbellata*, bears broad clusters of flowers 12 in. high and with a wide range of colours including white, pink, carmine-rose, purple, and lilac. A variety known as 'Rich Purple' is especially effective in a garden. Candytuft should be sown in masses as soon as the weather becomes genial about the end of March or early April. The plants prefer cool moist conditions when young and if the weather becomes hot, guard against flea beetle. A dwarf-growing group Dwarf Hybrids growing only 6–9 in. is very suitable for edgings and patches in the front of the annual border (Pl. 112).

I. amara from which the beautiful variety 'Improved White Spiral' (Pl. 113) originates, forms striking long spikes of pure white flowers 18 in. high. This also makes a good pot plant for the cold greenhouse.

Impatiens: Balsam; Tropical and Northern Temperate Regions; *Balsaminaceae.*

112. Candytuft (*Iberis umbellata*) 'Dwarf Carmine'.

113. Candytuft (*Iberis amara*) 'Improved White Spiral'.

I. balsamina is a tender annual from India and makes a showy summer-flowering plant where sufficient care can be given to its cultivation. It requires a rich soil, not lacking moisture, and a warm sunny situation. Sow in heat in March and plant out in June when all risk of frost is over. The best variety is Improved Camellia-flowered. 18 in., freely branching with masses of fully double camellia-like flowers in shades of pink, scarlet, violet, and white, during July and August. A dwarf form is particularly suitable for flowering in pots in the cool greenhouse.

I. holstii (Pl. 114) and *sultani* are tender perennials which are well worth growing as tender annuals in the greenhouse for summer decoration. They form free-flowering branching plants 1–1½ ft in a wide range of colours, including lilac, ruby, salmon-pink, and orange-scarlet. These plants will remain in flower for weeks on end and succeed admirably in the living-room. Sow in heat, March–April. Flower in 6-in. pots July–October.

114. Balsam (*Impatiens holstii*) Dwarf Orange-scarlet.

I. glandulifera (syn. *I. roylei*), a strong, rather coarse-growing hardy annual 5–6 ft, bearing conspicuous purple flowers, sometimes white, and doing well in shady borders. Naturalized in many parts of Great Britain and very decorative in woodland gardens.

Ionopsidium: Violet Cress; Portugal; *Cruciferae*.

I. acaule, an attractive H.A. for growing in crevices in a paved path, preferably in shady places. A tiny tufted plant only 2–3 in., covered with small violet-blue flowers. It frequently sows itself but never becomes a nuisance. Sow from the end of March to June in the open.

Ipomoea: Morning Glory; Tropical America; *Convolvulaceae*.

I. rubro-coerulea (*Pharbitis tricolor*), the true Morning Glory is a H.H.A. climber bearing large sky-blue flowers 4 in. across and flourishing in a warm sunny position. The place to see this plant as it should be grown is in a climate such as the French Riviera where it will grow 10 ft high and flower for months on end. In this country it is best grown under glass when it makes a delightful climber for the summer months. In really warm sunny positions it is well worth growing out of doors, when the variety 'praecox' should always be procured. Sow February–March, under glass and plant out when risk of frost is over. It is often an advantage to chip the seed before sowing.

I. coccinea: see **Quamoclit.**

Isatis: Woad; Europe including Britain; *Cruciferae*.

I. tinctoria – Woad. A hardy biennial, useful in the mixed border and for the cutting garden where the tall loose sprays of young fruits or seed pods are most attractive for decoration. 2–4 ft, foliage glaucous green, loose racemes of small yellow flowers, followed by flattened purple-brown seed pods.

Jacobaea: see **Senecio.**

Kaulfussia amelloides: see **Charieis heterophylla.**

Kochia: Summer Cypress; South France eastward to Japan; *Chenopodiaceae*.

K. scoparia trichophylla, a useful H.H.A. foliage plant, with a dense bushy habit, 2–3 ft high and fully 12 in. across (Pl. 115). The finely cut foliage is pale green and very ornamental, and the bushy plants stand upright without any support. In the

115. Summer Cypress, *Kochia scoparia*.

116. *Lavatera trimestris* 'Loveliness'.

207

autumn the leaves turn a rich coppery-red. Sow in April under glass taking care in watering the young seedlings which damp-off very easily. Plant out about the end of May.

Larkspur: see Chapter 6.

Lathyrus odoratus: see Chapter 6 under Sweet Pea.

Lavatera: Mallow; Mediterranean Region; *Malvaceae*.

L. trimestris (*rosea*) is a robust growing H.A., forming a branching plant 2–3 ft high and as much through (Pl. 116). The large pink mallow-like flowers are borne in great profusion and continue to open all through the summer. Sow in the open ground in April and thin to 12–15 in. apart in rows spaced 24–30 in. The best variety is 'Loveliness', a deep pink. There is also a pure white form. The flower stems are excellent for cutting. Lavateras may be planted in groups in the mixed border, in clumps in the annual border, and also make an excellent flowering hedge lasting the whole summer.

Layia: California; *Compositae*.

L. elegans, a useful H.A. for a sunny position with yellow flowers tipped with white. 12 in. (Pl. 117).

Leptosiphon hybridus: see **Gilia**.

Leptosyne: California; *Compositae*.

These plants are botanically placed under *Coreopsis*, but usually still known as *Leptosyne* in gardens.

L. maritima, Sea Dahlia. Easily flowered as a H.H.A. and from a sowing in March produces vigorous growing branching plants 2–3 ft bearing large golden-yellow flowers on long stems. A handsome plant. Excellent, too, as a pot plant for the cool greenhouse.

L. stillmanni. A very quick flowering H.A. with bright lemon-yellow flowers, very free-flowering, 12–15 in.

Limnanthes: California; *Limnanthaceae*.

L. douglasii. A charming H.A., forming a low-growing plant 6 in. high, with shiny green foliage and bearing open yellow flowers edged with white (Pl. 118). Beloved of bees. Very hardy and may be sown in the open in September when it will flower in April–June and any time in April–May to flower during the summer. Suitable for edgings, for patches in the rock garden, and for early flowers in the cold house.

117. *Layia elegans.*

118. *Limnanthes douglasii.*

119. Statice (*Limonium sinuatum*) 'Art Shades'.

Limonium: Sea Lavender, Statice; Mediterranean Area; *Plumbaginaceae.*

L. sinuatum. A biennial but best treated as a H.H.A. Many variations from the original blue and white coloured flowers are now available including pure white, rose, lavender, mauve, and dark blue. Many shades being offered separately. A mixture known as 'Art Shades' (Pl. 119) has a blend of unusual colours such as salmon-pink, orange-yellow, pink, and carmine. 18 in. to 2 ft, much grown for cutting and for treating as 'everlastings' for winter decoration.

L. bonduelli. A fine yellow flowered species.

120. *Limonium suworowii.*

L. suworowii. An annual much used for pot culture. The flowering scape rises above the rosette of foliage 18 in. to 2 ft, and makes an attractive pot plant for the cool greenhouse, remaining in flower for a long time (Pl. 120). Sow in March and pot on as required and finally into 5- or 6-in. pots. The bright rose flower spikes are much used for decoration as cut flowers and for table decoration.

Linaria: Toad Flax; Spain, Portugal, and Morocco; *Scrophulariaceae.*

L. maroccana. A widely grown H.A. Stems slender 9–15 in. ending in spikes of tiny snapdragon-like flowers in a very wide range of colouring including pure white, yellow, violet-purple, crimson, and mauve (Pl. 121). They make striking patches of colour in the mixed border, the rock garden, and in pots or pans in the cool greenhouse.

L. alpina. Alpine Toadflax. A hardy perennial but easily flowered as an annual. The dwarf spreading plant with glaucous green foliage bears violet-blue flowers with a bright orange patch on the lower lip.

Linum: Flax; North Africa, Europe; *Linaceae.*

L. grandiflorum var. *rubrum,* the 'Scarlet Flax' is one of the best of our hardy annuals. A slender growing plant 12–15 in. high, with soft green foliage. The stems end in loose heads of large red flowers (Pl. 122). The plants look best massed in groups in the mixed border or in beds by themselves. The petals have a silky sheen on them and rustle in a light breeze, making them particularly attractive. A white form of this variety is now available.

L. usitatissimum, Common Flax. Pale blue flowers carried on tall slender stems $1\frac{1}{2}$–2 ft high.

Lobelia, blue: see Chapter 6.

Lobularia, *maritima*: see *Alyssum maritimum.*

Lunaria: Honesty; Sweden; *Cruciferae.*

L. annua (biennis). A good biennial for the semi-wild garden, doing well in light shade. 18–24 in., flowers varying from white to pale purple and rich purple. When the seed is shed in autumn the empty silvery seed heads make a charming winter decoration. They should be gathered before being discoloured by too much rain. Sow in April and May for flowering the following year.

The rich purple form associates well with the common bluebell.

Lupinus: Lupin; America and Southern Europe; *Leguminosae.*

L. polyphyllus, the perennial lupin, owing to its ease of cultivation and wide range of colouring, is one of our best known

121. *Linaria maroccana.*

122. *Linum grandi-
florum* var. *rub-
rum*, the scarlet
flax.

garden plants. The finest form is the Russell Strain and if seed is sown from April to June, the seedlings will flower well the following year.

The truly annual species, however, should not be overlooked. Many of them are very useful flowering plants for the summer garden, flowering over a long period and with a wide range of colouring.

L. hartwegii. H.A. $1\frac{1}{2}$–$2\frac{1}{2}$ ft with spikes of white and pale blue flowers. Very useful annual.

L. luteus. H.A. $1\frac{1}{2}$–2 ft with rich yellow flowers, sweetly scented.

L. sub-carnosus (Texas Blue Bonnet). H.A. A dwarf-growing plant, 9–12 in., with rich blue flowers, succeeding well in poor dry soil. Sow in place in April and May.

L. mutabilis. H.A. Tall growing, 4–5 ft, with handsome spikes of flowers in shades of dark blue with yellow and rose markings on the wings, also pink and white and blue. Scented. A decorative plant for the mixed border deserving to be widely grown.

L. tricolor (*hybridus*). H.A. $1\frac{1}{2}$–2 ft, bushy, free-flowering plants of possibly hybrid origin with spikes of smallish flowers opening white and changing to pink (Pl. 123). Well worth growing.

Maize: see **Zea**.

Malcomia: see under **Virginian Stock**.

Matthiola: see Chapter 6 under Stocks.

Matricaria: North Temperate Regions; *Compositae*.

Although more often placed botanically under *Chrysanthemum* the plant is usually known in gardens under *Matricaria*.

M. eximia (*Chrysanthemum parthenium*). H.P. but flowered the first year from seed sown under glass in March. Two varieties, 'Golden Ball' and 'Silver Ball' (Pl. 124) are much used for bedding, for edgings, and for pot culture. Height 12 in., a compact-growing plant with flat heads of small double flowers, yellow and ivory white respectively.

M. maritima (*M. inodora*, *Chrysanthemum inodorum*). The double flowered form known as 'Bridal Robe' is a charming plant with deep green finely cut foliage and pure white double flowers. H.A. Excellent for cutting.

214

123. *Lupinus tricolor.*

124. *Matricaria eximia* 'Silver Ball'.

215

Mentzelia: California; *Loasaceae*.

M. lindleyi, better known in gardens as *Bartonia aurea*, 'Blazing Star'. An easily grown showy hardy annual 1½–2 ft high bearing large yellow flowers with a central mass of feathery stamens (Pl. 125). Sow March to April in open ground in full sun.

Mesembryanthemum: South Africa; *Aizoaceae*.

M. criniflorum (*Dorotheanthus bellidiflorus*). A useful low-growing half-hardy annual forming a spreading plant 4 in. high and bearing numerous daisy-like flowers 1–1½ in. across with a wide range of charming pastel colouring including white edged with crimson, pink, or buff, and self-coloured forms in shades of rose, yellow, apricot, and crimson (Pl. 126). Useful for edgings, irregular patches in sunny borders or the rock garden, and for pot culture in the cool greenhouse. Sow under glass in March and April and plant out in May.

Michauxia: Levant; *Campanulaceae*.

A handsome biennial. Sow in cold frame in September, and plant out in a warm sunny border in May. A branching plant 2–4 ft, bearing waxy white flowers distributed along the stem and branches, shaped somewhat like that of the Turk's-cap lily.

Mignonette: *Reseda odorata*; North Africa; *Resedaceae*.

This charming hardy annual with its unique fragrance appears to be grown less than formerly, which is a pity. It is one of the most delightful plants of the garden for cutting, for its fragrance outdoors, and for pot culture in the cool greenhouse. The culture is simple. The seed should not be buried, the soil must be firm and well drained with sufficient moisture, and there must be a sufficiency of lime.

The old-fashioned 'sweet-scented' strain is charming (Pl. 127). Some of the newer, larger flowered varieties are well worth growing also, such as 'Golden Goliath' and 'Crimson Giant'. Sow outside from April onwards and thin early: in August for pot culture, in September for spring flowering, and in January–March for summer flowering. Sow in June for late autumn and winter. Use a rich compost, thin early to 4–5 plants in a 6-in. pot, and feed with liquid manure when full of roots.

125. *Mentzelia lindleyi,*
often known in
gardens as
Bartonia aurea.

126. *Mesembryanthe-*
mum criniflorum.

127. Mignonette, *Reseda odorata.*

Mimulus: Monkey Flower; Western parts of North and South America; *Scrophulariaceae.*

Most of the garden forms have originated from the two species *M. cupreus* and *M. luteus,* and although perennial, are conveniently treated as H.H.A. The hybrid forms are very showy and are known variously as 'Giant Hybrids', 'Queen's Prize', 'Monarch' strain, and so on. Sow under glass in March, giving shade in the early stages. The seedlings grow quickly and produce branching plants 12–15 in. with large flowers of rich colouring including pink, crimson, and yellow, with many intermediate shades and spotted and blotched with contrasting colours. They may be planted out in a moist, semi-shaded position or make admirable pot plants for the cool greenhouse, flowering freely in June and July from a spring or slightly later sowing outside.

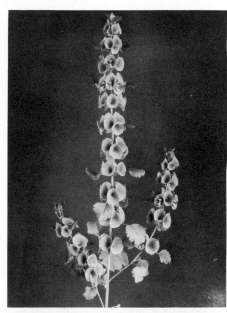

128. *Moluccella laevis*
(Bells of Ireland).
A fine plant for
decorative
arrangements.

129. *Moluccella laevis*,
dried flowering
spikes.

Mina lobata: see **Quamoclit lobata**.

Moluccella laevis: Molucca Balm, Bells of Ireland; Mediterranean;
 Labiatae (Pls 128 and 129), see also p. 43.

A hardy annual more grown in the United States of America
than in this country. Succeeds best grown singly in pots under
glass in a light compost. Sow March–April. The plants will
then form tall spikes of flowers, 18–30 in. long. The small white
flowers are produced in successive whorls in the axils of the
bright green nettle-like leaves, but it is the enlarged calyces
which are decorative. They are large, cup-shaped, pale sea-
green and beautifully netted and veined.

When using the fresh spikes for decoration it is better to
remove the axillary leaves, leaving the beautiful calyces by
themselves, or they may be left to ripen in late summer when
the spikes turn an attractive ivory colour and are most useful
for winter decoration.

Myosotis: Forget-me-not; Europe including Britain; *Boraginaceae*.
The many garden forms of this popular plant come mostly from
 M. alpestris, and are best treated as hardy biennials. The forms
available coming true from seed range from quite dwarf plants
only a few inches high to vigorous branching plants 12–15 in.
high and as much across. The colours include white, pink, pale
blue, and rich blue. Sow from May to June and plant out into
flowering position in autumn. There are also varieties particularly suitable for pot culture. These may be sown in June and
July for flowering in the cool greenhouse during the winter.

This is a most useful plant for spring bedding with bulbs or
for making drifts of colour in the semi-wild garden in light
woodland.

Nasturtium: see Chapter 6.

Nemesia: see Chapter 6.

Nemophila: California; *Hydrophyllaceae*.
Nemophilas are among the best of the hardy annuals from
California. The most widely grown is *N. menziesii* var. *insignis*
(Pl. 130). The slender-growing spreading plant grows to a
height of 6–8 in. and is covered during summer with sky blue
flowers with a white eye. Useful for edging, patches in the
annual border, or the rock garden. Will stand light shade and

130. *Nemophila menziesii* var. *insignis*.

thrive in a moist cool situation. Various forms are also available, including pure white, deep purple, and spotted. Sow in the open ground in March or April for summer flowering, and in favourable situations in autumn for spring flowering. Suitable also for pot culture in the cool greenhouse.

Nicotiana: Tobacco; Tropical America; *Solanaceae*.

N. alata (*affinis*), strictly a perennial, and persisting in very sheltered situations, but best treated as a H.H.A. Sow under glass in March and do not plant out until risk of frost is over. This species has white flowers tinged with violet closed during the day but open in the evening and then sweetly scented. Vigorous branching plants 3 ft, flowering from July to September. They like a rich well-cultivated soil and as long as the soil is enriched and adequately watered will thrive under tall trees, when because of the shade, the flowers will remain open. Other colours are available including pink, red, and crimson, and dwarfer growing forms, 'Crimson Bedder', and 'Dwarf White Bedder'.

'Sensation Mixed' (Pl. 131), derived from a hybrid between *N. alata* and *N. langsdorfii*, has flowers smaller than *alata* but remaining mainly open during the day and worth growing on that account. The attractive range of colours includes pale green and smoky purple.

N. suaveolens is a very sweet scented annual species from Australia with slender stems and rather beautiful small pure white flowers. A particularly good pot plant, sometimes offered as 'Miniature White'.

Nierembergia: Cup Flower; South America; *Solanaceae*.

N. caerulea (*hippomanica*) (Pl. 132) is a nearly hardy perennial best treated as a H.H.A. in this country. From seed sown under glass in February plants may be planted out in May and will flower during the summer months. The bushy, upright growing plants 6–9 in. produce an abundance of small flattish petunia-like flowers, violet-blue in colour. Particularly useful for sunny patches in the rock garden or the front of the annual border, also making attractive pot plants. The plants can easily be preserved in the cool house or even cold frame with some protection in winter and will flower again from May onwards.

Nigella: Love-in-a-Mist; Europe and North Africa; *Ranunculaceae*.

N. damascena, the best known variety is 'Miss Jekyll' (Pl. 133), which has large semi-double flowers of cornflower blue. This is an attractive upright growing plant 12–18 in. with deep green finely cut foliage. It is one of the best of our hardy annuals and may be sown in September in open well-drained situations where it will stand most winters and will then form strong branching plants 18 in. to 2 ft, coming into flower towards the end of May. Can also be sown in March and April when the plants flower a little later and are not quite so vigorous. Excellent for cut flowers and for growing in pots in the cold house. The seed pods are conspicuous with persistent stigmas resembling horns and are much used for decorative purposes. There is a deep blue form and a white.

N. hispanica – similar to above but with grey stems and foliage and violet-coloured flowers with attractive red-coloured stamens. The seed pods are also very decorative.

131. *Nicotiana alata* 'Sensation Mixed'.

132. *Nierembergia caerulea*.

Oenothera: Evening Primrose; Temperate Regions of North and South America; *Onagraceae*.

O. biennis. The Common Evening Primrose is a well-known biennial, very useful for the wild garden, where it will frequently sow itself freely. It will do well in light shade. The best form is one selected for its bright red flower stems and calyces. Sow in June–July for flowering the following year in May and June. Height 2–4 ft.

O. acaulis (taraxacifolia). A trailing species with prominent large flowers opening white shading to rose; there is also a yellow form. Treat as a H.H.A. Very useful in the rock garden.

O. odorata. A biennial which may be treated as a hardy annual. Slender stems 2–3 ft high with primrose-coloured flowers and reddish-coloured flower stem. Only opening in the evening.

O. trichocalyx. A biennial from California best grown in this country as a H.H.A. Sow in March under glass and plant out in full sun in May. The grey-leaved plants grow to a height of 12–18 in. and are freely branched. The flowers are a beautiful pure white admirably shown off by the whitish stems and grey foliage. The flowers besides being sweetly scented have the added advantage of remaining open during the day. Good for cutting.

Omphalodes linifolia: see **Venus's Navelwort**.

Onopordon: see **Thistle, Giant**.

Pansy: see **Viola**.

Papaver: see Chapter 6 under Poppies.

Pea, Sweet: see Chapter 6.

Penstemon: North America; *Scrophulariaceae*.

The best border forms have been raised from crosses between probably *P. hartwegii* and *P. cobaea*. If sown under glass in March and April and planted out in May these hybrids make branching free-flowering plants 18 in. to 2 ft, coming into flower at the end of July and continuing until September. The plants, in a great variety of shades coming true from seed, are literally covered with flowering spikes (Pl. 134). The colours include white, shades of pink, scarlet, crimson, and purple. Many of the tubular flowers are edged with contrasting shades.

133. Love-in-a-Mist
(*Nigella damas-
cena*) 'Miss Jekyll'.

134. Penstemons,
large-flowered
mixed.

225

The plants are not absolutely hardy but will frequently persist for some years in open well-drained positions and will then flower the following year somewhat earlier.

Petunia: see Chapter 6.

Phacelia: California; *Hydrophyllaceae*.

P. campanularia. One of our most striking hardy annuals. Attractive greyish foliage, 8–9 in., the slender stems ending in clusters of bell-shaped flowers deep gentian-blue in colour with prominent primrose-coloured anthers. Beloved of bees. Suitable for edging, patches in the rock garden, and for pots. Sow in March and April in place and in favourable situations in September.

P. viscida (*Eutoca viscida*). One of the good blue-flowered hardy annuals, taller than above reaching a height of 1–2 ft and with fresh green foliage.

P. tanacetifolia. A tall species with curled flower heads of soft lavender-blue 1½–2½ ft. Much grown for bees.

Pharbitis: see **Ipomoea.**

Phlox, annual: see Chapter 6.

Platystemon: Cream Cups; California; *Papaveraceae*.

P. californicus. A charming grey-leaved hardy annual with small poppy-like cream-coloured flowers borne on 9–10 in. stalks rising above a mat of foliage. Particularly suitable for autumn sowing and frequently sowing itself in the garden but never obtrusively.

Polyanthus: Europe including Britain; *Primulaceae*.

The garden polyanthus originated from a cross between the primrose *Primula vulgaris* and the cowslip *Primula veris* and of recent years great improvements have been achieved both in habit, range of colouring, and size of flower (Pl. 135). Great credit for this work must be given to Mr Alan Langdon of Bath. The colours now include, beside the original yellow, pure white, pinks, crimsons, flame colours, and blue, many of which come true from seed. Excellent for cut flowers. The simplest and best method of raising polyanthus is undoubtedly from seed and this is best sown in a cool greenhouse in February–March in a light compost with leaf soil. On germination place in a cold frame where the seedlings may be shaded

135. Polyanthus, a fine mixed strain growing under flowering crab-
apples and cherries in Buckinghamshire.

and keep cool and moist. Prick off as soon as they can be
handled, about 1 in. apart in frames or boxes, and by mid-May
onwards the young seedlings may be pricked out in a cool
shady situation out of doors. Good flowering plants will be
ready for planting into their flowering position in October. To
get extra strong plants a sowing may be made in September in
cold frames, prick out either direct into frames or trays, and
transfer the seedlings into a shady position outside in April.
These will make extra large flowering plants for planting the
following October, to come into flower the next spring. Polyanthuses are widely used in the garden. They are particularly
beautiful in drifts under fruit trees or other spring flowering
ornamental trees. They may also be used in formal bedding by
themselves or with bulbs, for cut flowers, and for pot plants
in the cool greenhouse, and for decoration in the house.

Poppies: see Chapter 6.

Portulaca: Sun Plant; South America; **Portulaceae.**

P. grandiflora is a low-growing H.A. suitable for a hot sunny situation. The spreading plant, 6–8 in. high, bears cup-shaped flowers, both single and double, opening in sunshine and with a wide range of colouring. The mixture includes white, rose and white, rosy-purple, sulphur-yellow, and orange-scarlet. It is excellent for carpeting a hot sunny bank or planting in shallow stone bowls or other receptacles. Sow the seed in gentle heat in March. Care must be taken in transplanting. Seed may also be sown in place in May and June, when the risks of transplanting are avoided.

Primrose:

Primula vulgaris. Like the garden polyanthus, the garden forms of the 'Common primrose' have been greatly improved in recent years particularly in regard to the range of colours available. In dappled sunshine, say under fruit trees, a drift of mixed coloured primroses is a beautiful sight. Excellent in bowls as cut flowers. Use the same methods of cultivation as recommended for polyanthus.

Auricula. Border or Alpine auriculas will grow to perfection in any good garden loam and are easily raised from seed. The seed may be sown somewhat later than as recommended for polyanthus but otherwise the cultivation is similar. Auriculas will stand rather more sun than polyanthuses and may be planted near a window so that their delicious fragrance may come into the house. From a good strain of seed, the range of colour is beautiful including crimson-maroon, purple-maroon, lilac, clear yellow, and mauve. Excellent for cutting.

Primula: *malacoides*: see Chapter 3, p. 54.

Quamoclit: Central America; *Convolvulaceae.*

Mostly twining annuals from Central America and only suitable for very sheltered positions outdoors. In sheltered verandas however and the cool greenhouse they make attractive climbers growing 8–10 ft. Sow in small pots under glass in March and April, and pot on as required. Plant outside in June in rich soil.

136. *Rudbeckia bicolor* 'Golden Sunset'.

Q. coccinea (*Ipomoea coccinea*). Fragrant scarlet flowers with yellow throat in August and September.

Q. lobata (*Mina lobata*). Vigorous free-flowering climber well worth trying in sunny sheltered positions out of doors, as well as under glass. The flowers open bright crimson, soon changing to orange-yellow and finally to creamy-white.

Q. pinnata (*Ipomaea quamoclit*). Cypress Vine, a beautiful climber with finely divided foliage and tubular scarlet flowers.

Reseda: see **Mignonette.**

Ricinus communis: Castor Oil Plant; Tropical Africa; *Euphorbiaceae.*

A handsome foliage plant. The plants grow rapidly in favourable situations reaching to a height of 6–8 ft with large palmately lobed leaves up to 2 ft across and large seed pods covered with soft spines. *R. gibsoni* is a dwarfer growing type with bronze-tinted stems and foliage. Treat as a H.H.A. Sow the seed singly in small pots under glass in March in a temperature of 60° F. Pot on as required and gradually harden off for planting out in June.

Rudbeckia: Coneflower; North America; *Compositae.*

R. bicolor. A showy annual species best treated as a H.H.A., 1½ ft, with flower heads borne on long stalks, excellent for cutting. The petals are tipped with yellow, with a central zone of mahogany-crimson and the central disc dark brown (Pl. 136). The plant comes into flower in late summer and autumn. Sow under glass in March and plant out in May.

R. hirta. This is a hardy biennial species but can also be flowered as a H.H.A. The best form is that known as 'Hirta Hybrida'. This forms vigorous plants bearing flower heads on stalks 2–3 ft long. The flowers often measure 3–4 in. across and are borne during summer and autumn in great profusion. The colours include clear lemon-yellow, orange, and bronze and some approaching rich crimson, many with beautiful contrasting zones of colour. Excellent for cutting. Sow under glass in February or March, plant out in May to flower the same year, or during June and July to flower the following year.

Salpiglossis: Chile; *Solanaceae.*

S. sinuata. A very beautiful half-hardy annual with rich

137. *Salpiglossis sinuata* 'Sutton's Triumph'.

coloured tubular flowers in a wide variety of brilliant colouring (Pl. 137). The plants in the open will grow 2½–3 ft, and in pots 3½–4½ ft. The colour range is remarkable, including ivory and gold, golden-yellow, chamois, rose-crimson and gold, crimson gold-veined, rich crimson, scarlet and gold, blue and gold, and rich violet. Many flowers are beautifully veined with contrasting colours. The mixed hybrids make a beautiful mixture, the best strain being one known as 'Sutton's Triumph'. Many separate colours are also available true from seed.

The flowers are excellent for cutting.

Sow the seed under glass at the end of February or during March and prick off into small pots from which they can be planted out at the end of May or early June. Seed may also be sown in the open ground at the end of April and May. Choose a rich, well-drained soil and a sheltered sunny situation. They do not stand wind and must have warmth. It is very important to see that the plants are kept growing and never receive a check at any time especially in the early stages. Flowers will begin to show at the end of June and continue for 6–8 weeks.

Salpiglossis also make excellent pot plants. They must have heat, say 50–55° F. in the winter. Sow in August and September and pot the seedlings into 3-in. pots in a rich fibrous loam and well drained. Keep growing and avoid over-watering during the dead of winter. Give all light possible. Pot on as the plants grow, finally into 5-in. pots when they will flower in May and June. The main secret in successful cultivation is careful watering. Never allow the plants to become dry, on the other hand do not over-water especially when growth is slow. Seed may also be sown in heat in February and March for flowering in June and July.

Salvia: Mexico, California, and Brazil; *Labiatae*.

Several species of salvia make most useful garden annuals. One of the best known being a tender perennial from Brazil.

S. splendens, the Scarlet Sage. Treated as a H.H.A. by being sown under glass in February and March, potted on singly, and planted out early June, the early flowering forms come into flower in July and remain throughout the summer into the autumn months. The earliest variety is a dwarf-growing compact plant 9–12 in., 'Blaze of Fire', followed by 'Fireball' and 'Harbinger', somewhat taller. The colour is vivid scarlet and therefore the plants must be placed with care. They can be very effective especially in late summer and early autumn in a patch or bed by themselves surrounded by green grass or a background of trees. Purple and violet-blue can be satisfactorily associated with them and the petunia known as 'Blue Bedder' associates well. Other colours are now making their appearance such as rose-pink and violet.

S. farinacea. Another perennial species but best treated as a H.H.A. Particularly attractive, 2–3 ft, with shiny bright green leaves and long spikes of lavender-blue flowers, whose calyces are densely covered with short white hairs giving a charming contrast to the lavender-blue flowers. The plants flower the whole summer from July onwards. There is a deeper coloured form known as 'Blue Bedder'.

S. horminum, Blue Beard. A H.A. from South Europe producing bushy plants 1–1½ ft, the stems terminating in spikes of small flowers with deep violet-blue floral bracts. The pink form 'Pink Lady' associates with this well.

S. patens. Another tender perennial easily grown as a H.H.A. having spikes of brilliant blue flowers 1½ ft long. It is rather a loose-growing plant but the flowers are such a vivid blue that it is worth growing on that account. There is a pale blue form known as 'Cambridge Blue'.

Saponaria: Soapwort; Europe; *Caryophyllaceae.*

S. calabrica. A dwarf-growing H.A. bearing starry pink flowers in great profusion 6–12 in. Sow in place in spring or autumn in full sun.

S. vaccaria (Vaccaria vulgaris). A popular H.A. much used for cutting, bearing sprays of pink flowers, 2–3 ft. There is also a pure white form. Sow in place in spring and autumn in full sun.

Scabiosa: see Chapter 6 under Annual Scabious.

Schizanthus: see Chapter 6.

Sedum coeruleum: Southern Europe and Algeria; *Crassulaceae.*

A charming little H.H.A. only 3–4 in., with bright glossy green succulent leaves and compact habit. Easily raised from seed,

233

sown in gentle heat in March or April and planted out in May. The plant is covered with a profusion of small pale blue flowers during summer when the foliage turns a bronzy-red. Very useful for the rock garden and for the crevices in paving.

Senecio : Annual Cineraria, Jacobaea; S. Africa; *Compositae*.

(For notes on the true Cineraria, *Senecio cruentus*, see under Cineraria.) *S. arenarius* (Annual Cineraria). A native of South Africa and should be treated as a H.H.A., being sown in March and planted out in May in an open well-drained situation. Produces branching plants 12 in. bearing masses of tiny cineraria-like single flowers in a wide range of colouring including shades of lavender-mauve, rosy lavender, pale yellow, and apricot. Some of the bronzy-apricot shades are quite unusual. A good plant for the rock garden, the annual border, and cutting.

S. elegans (*Jacobaea elegans*). Usually offered in seed lists under Jacobaea. The original plant has single flowers reddish-purple with a prominent yellow centre and was introduced over 150 years ago. Bright rose and purple magenta strains will come true from seed and also double forms, useful for cutting, 18 in. to 2 ft. H.A., can be sown under glass in March and planted out in May, or in the open ground in April.

Shortia californica : see **Baeria.**

Silene : Catchfly; Southern Europe and South Africa; *Caryophyllaceae*.

The silenes are useful hardy annuals which appear to have rather gone out of favour. The varieties of *S. pendula* in shades of white, pink, salmon, lilac, and crimson, with both double and single flowers, form close growing plants 6–8 in., covered with flowers in spring if sown in place in the autumn. If the soil is apt to be cold and wet in the winter, they should be wintered in cold frames and planted out in April. They make a good groundwork for wallflowers and spring flowering bulbs. Sow also in place in spring.

S. armeria. An old-fashioned hardy annual with blue-green foliage and heads of bright rose-pink flowers. 12–15 in. This species will naturalize itself on old walls and may be sown in the autumn or spring.

138. Swan River Daisy, *Brachycome iberidifolia*.

S. fuscata (*pseudo-atocion*). Makes a bushy, free-flowering plant with starry bright pink flowers, 9–12 in. Flowers in spring from an autumn sowing.

S. oculata: see **Viscaria**.

Specularia speculum: see **Venus's Looking-Glass.**

Statice: see **Limonium.**

Stocks: see Chapter 6.

Virginian: see under **Virginian Stock.**

Swan River Daisy, *Brachycome iberidifolia*: Australia; *Compositae*.

A delightful Australian annual which can be sown in place in April or under glass in March and planted out in May. The small branching plants, 9–12 in., bear on the end of wiry stems masses of flowers resembling miniature cinerarias, in shades of mauve, blue, pale blue, rose-pink, purple, and pure white

(Pl. 138). The plants come into flower in June and remain in full flower for several weeks. Very useful as edging and in patches in front of the annual border and for placing in bowls as cut flowers. Also particularly useful as pot plants for the greenhouse in summer and for bringing into the dwelling house. Sown in February and potted on finally into 5-in. pots, Swan River Daisies will make plants 12–18 in. high and 12 in. across, covered in bloom for three months during the summer. Under glass the flowers are delicately scented.

Sweet Pea: see Chapter 6.

Sweet Rocket: Europe; *Cruciferae*.

Hesperis matronalis. A charming hardy biennial for the wild garden easily raised from seed sown in May and June for flowering the following year. The long flower spikes grow 2–3 ft in height and are fragrant in the evening. Colour purple, white, and delicate mauve.

H. tristis. Another charming hardy biennial, 18 in., flowers whitish or cream, brownish-red or purple. Very fragrant at night. A useful plant for the wild garden and naturalizing on old walls.

Sweet Sultan: see under *Centaurea moschata*.

Sweet William, *Dianthus barbatus*; Europe; *Caryophyllaceae*.

A well-known perennial plant best treated as a hardy biennial in gardens. Well-grown plants reach 2–3 ft in height and 18 in. across. They come into flower in June and make very decorative subjects for the mixed border and for cutting. Many colours are available true from seed including pure white, shades of pink, scarlet, and crimson. A mixture known as 'Bright Auricula-eyed' has a particularly rich range of colouring. A dwarf strain is also available.

For a description of the annual form see under **Dianthus**.

Tagetes: see Chapter 6 under African and French Marigolds.

Thistle, Giant: *Onopordon acanthium*; Europe; *Compositae*.

A handsome hardy biennial growing 8–10 ft with large spiny leaves. The whole plant, stem and leaves, is covered with fine white hairs giving a very decorative effect. The large flower heads are blue-purple. Sow the seed in the open ground in May and June for flowering the following year (Pl. 139).

139. Giant Thistle, *Onopordon acanthium.*

Tithonia: Mexican Sunflower; *Compositae.*

T.rotundifolia (*T. speciosa*). A tall-growing vigorous plant useful for the mixed border or semi-wild garden in autumn. The plant is much branched, 5–6 ft, and flowers in August and September. The flowers resemble a single dahlia, the rich orange-red petals being neatly arranged. A striking colour and good for cutting. Sow the seed at the end of March under glass and pot on singly as for dahlias, planting out only after all risk of frost is over.

As this is very definitely a short-day plant, an interesting experiment can be made in any garden. In the end of April or early May, whenever the days lengthen, cover the young seedlings in pots with an empty over-turned box at, say, 5 p.m. and uncover at 8 a.m. in order to shorten the length of daylight. These plants so treated will flower at the end of June and remain only 3–3½ ft high. A variety 'Torch' has recently been introduced from America and is dwarfer growing than the type.

Torenia: Wish-bone Flower; Tropics; *Scrophulariaceae.*

T.fournieri. A tender greenhouse annual, easily grown in a cool greenhouse. Sow the seed in March in a temperature of about 60° F. Prick out and keep in warm moist conditions till large enough to pot on singly. The final potting may be made in 5-in. pots and the night temperature may be slightly cooler. 9–12 in., may need some support. The flowers appear in July and somewhat resemble an antirrhinum in shape, being violet and pale blue in colour with a golden-yellow blotch in the throat. Very free-flowering and most decorative, remaining in flower for 6–8 weeks. They are also useful for hanging baskets.

Trachelium coeruleum: Mediterranean; *Campanulaceae.*

A half-hardy perennial which by sowing under glass in spring will flower in sheltered positions out of doors in late summer and autumn the same year. Makes a splendid pot plant for the cool greenhouse, especially if it is kept for the following season, where frost can be excluded during the winter. It will then form a plant fully 3 ft high bearing decorative broad panicles of lavender-blue flowers.

Trachymene coerulea: Lace Flower; Western Australia; *Umbelliferae.*

A H.H.A. better known in gardens as *Didiscus caeruleus.*

238

140. *Ursinia anethoides.*

Makes an attractive pot plant for the cool greenhouse in late summer, useful for cut flowers and may be flowered outside successfully in warm sheltered situations. 1½–2 ft with lavender-blue flower heads on long stems. Sow under glass in March.

Tropaeolum: see Chapter 6 under Nasturtium.

Ursinia: South Africa; *Compositae*.

Showy H.H.A. useful in the annual border, for mixed planting, for cut flowers, and for pot work. They were formerly known under the name *Sphenogyne*.

U. anethoides. Probably the most widely grown in gardens. 15–18 in. with bushy, free-flowering habit and deep green finely cut foliage. The flower heads appear in July and August, brilliant orange with crimson-purple zone (Pl. 140). Sow March or April under glass and plant out in May.

239

Other species worth growing are *U. pulchra*, bright orange, 9 in., and *U. pygmaea*, rich orange, 6 in. A variety known as 'Golden Bedder' grows 9 in. high with golden-orange flower heads with deeper orange zone and free-flowering, bushy habit. A mixture offered under the name *U.* Hybrids includes a wide range of orange and lemon tones.

Venidio-Arctotis Hybrids: see under **Arctotis.**

Venidium: Namaqualand Daisy; South Africa; *Compositae.*

V. fastuosum. A showy half-hardy annual, with large rich orange flower heads and purple-black zone and shiny black centres, borne on long flower stalks (Pl. 141). The plants grow strongly to a height of 2–3 ft and 18 in. to 2 ft across. The whole plant is covered with fine white hairs giving it a woolly appearance. They must be grown in full sun and do best in a good loam, well drained. Sow in March under glass and plant out end of May.

V. fastuosum Hybrids. These have the habit of *fastuosum* and the colour range includes ivory, cream, yellow, and straw tinged with buff. These colours are well set off by the shiny black centres and maroon markings at the base of the ray petals.

Venidium 'Sutton's Dwarf Hybrids'. An interesting fertile interspecific hybrid – *V. calendulaceum* × *V. fastuosum.* The result is a plant intermediate between the two parents in every respect, a good garden plant flowering freely all summer in an open sunny situation. Flowers glowing orange with crimson zone at base of petals (Pl. 142). 15–18 in., spreading plant 18 in. across.

Venus's Looking-Glass: Mediterranean region; *Campanulaceae.*

A charming H.A. – *Specularia speculum*, easily grown and most useful as edging, patches in the rock garden, or annual border. Sown in place in April, thinly as the seed is very fine, the slender plants rise to 9–12 in. being covered with small violet-blue flowers lasting several weeks in flower. There is a white-flowered variety.

Venus's Navelwort: Portugal and Spain; *Boraginaceae.*

A delightful hardy annual, *Omphalodes linifolia.* The bushy

240

141. *Venidium fastuosum.*

grey-foliaged plants, 9–12 in., bear masses of small forget-me-not-like flowers, chalk-white in colour matching beautifully with the foliage. Can also be sown in autumn. Useful for the rock garden, edgings, cracks in stone paths, and in pots in the cool greenhouse.

Verbascum: Mullein; South Europe and Levant; *Scrophulariaceae.*

The Mulleins are mostly hardy biennials and include some handsome garden plants, suitable for the mixed border and in drifts in the wild garden, and light woodland.

V. olympicum. A noble biennial plant, 6–9 ft with long spikes of sulphur flowers. A large rosette of silvery foliage above which arise the handsome spikes of flowers in June.

V. bombyciferum. Sometimes offered under *V.* 'Broussa', a decorative hardy biennial which may be sown in place in June and July to flower the following summer. The whole plant and flower spikes are covered by a dense mat of fine white hairs, giving a very striking appearance (Pl. 143). In full sun and a well-drained position, the woolly winter rosette of large leaves is very decorative. The tall narrow dense flower spikes rise to 5–6 ft, the lemon flowers being a delightful contrast to the white woolly background.

The flower spikes require no staking and will stand quite high winds. This plant is therefore doubly useful and can be grown quite close to a windy shore. The spikes and woolly leaves are much used in indoor decoration.

V. 'Miss Wilmott' is a hybrid with pure white flowers 5–6 ft high. H.B.

V. 'Harkness Hybrid' is similar to above with pure yellow flowers continuing most of the summer. H.B.

V. phoeniceum is a hardy perennial, easily grown as a hardy biennial which will flower both in the open and in light shade if given enough moisture. The flower spikes are slender, 2–3 ft, the colours including a wide range of cool pastel shades, mauve, pink, purple, blue and white.

Verbena: see Chapter 6.

Viola: Pansies and Violas; *Violaceae.*

Pansies and violas are best treated in gardens as hardy biennials,

142. Venidium 'Sutton's Dwarf Hybrids'.

143. *Verbascum bombyciferum.*

being sown in June and July for flowering from early summer onwards the following year. The seed is preferably sown in a cold frame where it can be kept cool and moist and when seedlings are large enough pricked out in nursery lines in the open in showery weather 9–12 in. apart and 6 in. apart in the rows. Should the weather be hot and dry, draw shallow drills and water thoroughly before pricking out. In most districts plant out into flowering position in the autumn.

Pansies are delightful in mixture, and may be planted in beds by themselves or as groundwork for other plants. Besides the richness of colouring, the sweet cool fragrance, especially in early morning when the dew is on the plants is most refreshing. Many good mixtures are available, ranging from extra large bloom to those of more moderate dimensions. Many separate colours can also be obtained true from seed, most useful for definite colour schemes. A group known as 'Winter-flowering' which can be grown in mixture or in separate colours is perfectly hardy and will flower in favourable situations during winter and early spring. Pansies will also thrive in light shade.

Violas are very similar to Pansies in appearance and culture but are usually more tufted in habit and the flowers smaller and often self coloured. Again mixtures and separate colours are available, a mixture known as 'Fancy Shades' is very attractive, many plants bearing old-fashioned 'faced' flowers. Miniature and Tufted Violas, as their names imply, form compact low-growing plants covered with small flowers borne on tiny stalks. These have a wide range of colouring and are particularly useful for edgings and in the rock garden (Pl. 145).

Virginian Stock, *Malcomia maritima*: Southern Europe; *Cruciferae*.

A particularly delightful low-growing annual best grown in mixture, the colours of which include lilac, red, and white, the petals often being distinctively veined. The seed may be sown in place either in spring or autumn, and the tiny plants fit charmingly into cracks in paving or brick paths where they will often succeed in shaded places. Also particularly suitable for children's gardens. 6–9 in.

Viscaria, *Silene oculata*: *Caryophyllaceae*.

144. Pansies, a giant variety.

145. Viola, a good bedding variety.

One of the most beautiful of hardy annuals with a wide range
of colouring. These include pure white, shades of pink, red,
and carmine, pale blue and rich delphinium blue. It is very
beautiful grown in mixture or in special colour schemes,
12–15 in., dwarfer-growing varieties only 6 in. high are also
offered. Viscarias make charming pot subjects in the cool house
and will flower in early summer from a September sowing.

Wallflower: see Chapter 6.

Woad: see **Isatis**.

Zea Maize: *Gramineae*.

The varieties of ornamental maize with striped and variously
coloured foliage are most useful for interplanting with other
plants for their decorative effect and for use as cut foliage. The
strain known as 'Japonica' has narrow green foliage striped
yellow, creamy-white, and occasionally pink. 'Quadricolor'
has foliage striped with cream, rose, and purple, as well as
green and white. Sow in heat in March and April or in the open
in May. Plant out when danger of frost is over. 3–4 ft.

Zinnia: see Chapter 6.

Appendices

APPENDIX A · Annuals Suitable for Autumn Sowing in the Open

Calendula
Candytuft
Clarkia
Cornflower
Eschscholzia
Godetia
Larkspur
Limnanthes
Linaria
Nigella
Platystemon
Poppy – Annual
Scabious – Annual
Silene
Sweet Pea

APPENDIX B · Annuals and Biennials for Partial Shade

Ageratum
Aquilegia
Asperula
Begonia
Bellis (Double Daisy)
Campanula (including Canterbury bell)
Catananche
Collinsia
Coreopsis
Cynoglossum
Digitalis (Foxglove)
Impatiens glandulifera
Linum
Lupinus
Meconopsis
Mimulus
Myosotis (Forget-me-not)
Nemophila
Oenothera (Evening Primrose)
Pansy
Phlox drummondii
Polyanthus
Saponaria ocymoides
Sweet Rocket (Hesperis)
Verbascum phoeniceum
Viola

APPENDIX C · Annuals and Biennials for Covering Rough Banks and Similar Positions

Agrostemma githago 'Milas'
Arnebia
Borago officinalis
Calendula
Chrysanthemum – Annual
Convolvulus major
Convolvulus minor
Coreopsis
Cornflower
Echium plantagineum
Eschscholzia
Evening Primrose (Oenothera)
Lavatera
Limnanthes
Linaria
Linum grandiflorum
Lupins – Annual
Mentzelia aurea (Bartonia)
Nasturtium – Tall
Nasturtium – Dwarf
Nigella
Platystemon
Poppy, Opium
Poppy, Shirley
Silene
Sunflower
Virginian Stock

247

APPENDIX D · Annual Climbers

Canary Creeper
(Tropaeolum)
Cobaea scandens
Convolvulus major
Eccremocarpus
scaber

Humulus japonicus
– Annual Hop
Ipomoea rubro-coeru-
lea – Morning Glory
Maurandya scandens
Nasturtium – Tall
(Tropaeolum)

Ornamental Gourd
(Cucurbita)
Quamoclit lobata
(Mina lobata)
Sweet Pea
Thunbergia

APPENDIX E · Annuals Suitable for the Rock Garden

Adonis aestivalis and
A. annua
Alyssum
Anagallis
Antirrhinum, Rock
Hybrids and Little
Gem
Asperula
Calandrinia
umbellata
Charieis (Kaulfussia)
Collinsia bicolor
Cotula barbata
Cuphea
Delphinium
grandiflorum
Dimorphotheca
Emilia (Cacalia)
Erysimum

Eschscholzia
caespitosa
Felicia
Gazania
Gilia × hybrida (Lep-
tosiphon hybridus)
Godetia, dwarf
mauve
Helipterum (Acro-
clinium)
Ionopsidium acaule
Limnanthes
Linaria
Linum grandiflorum
Mesembryanthemum
criniflorum
(Dorotheanthus)
Nemesia
Nemophila

Nierembergia
Phacelia campanu-
laria
Platystemon califor-
nicus
Portulaca
Swan River Daisy
(Brachycome)
Ursinia
Venus's Looking-
Glass (Campanula
speculum)
Verbena
Viola – (Miniature
varieties)
Virginian Stock
Viscaria (Lychnis)

APPENDIX F · Annuals and Biennials Suitable for
Cutting

Amaranthus cauda-
tus (Love-lies-
bleeding)

Arctotis
Aster (Callistephus)
Calendula

Carnation Mar-
guerite (outdoor
and under glass)

Chrysanthemum – Annual
Chrysanthemum indicum – Cascade and Charm under glass
Clarkia
Coreopsis
Cornflower
Cosmea
Dahlia
Delphinium
Digitalis (Foxglove)
Dimorphotheca
Emilia (Cacalia)
Godetia
Gypsophila
Helichrysum (Ever-lastings)
Helipterum (Acro-clinium)

Honesty
Jacobaea
Larkspur
Lavatera
Limonium (Statice)
Linaria
Marigold
Mignonette
Moluccella (Bells of Ireland) (and under glass)
Myosotis (Forget-me-not)
Nasturtium
Nemesia
Nigella
Polyanthus
Poppies – Annual
Primula malacoides (under glass)
Rudbeckia

Salpiglossis
Scabious
Schizanthus (under glass)
Senecio arenarius (Annual cineraria)
Stocks (both outdoor and under glass)
Sunflower
Swan River Daisy (Brachycome)
Sweet Pea (outdoors and under glass)
Sweet Rocket
Sweet William
Viscaria
Wallflower
Zinnia

APPENDIX G · Annuals and Biennials for Flower Decoration

In addition to the plants recommended for the cutting garden, these are added here because of their beautiful foliage and fruits (seed heads).

Amaranthus
Artemisia
Atriplex
Cannabis sativa
Centaurea cineraria
Centaurea gymno-carpa
Eryngium
Euphorbia marginata
Fennel

Humea elegans
Humulus
Isatis
Kale – variegated
Kochia
Mesembryanthemum cordifolium varie-gatum
Mesembryanthemum crystallinum

Moluccella laevis
Papaver somniferum
Perilla
Physalis
Ricinus
Silybum marianum
Verbascum bombyci-ferum
Zea Maize, varie-gated

APPENDIX H · Annuals and Biennials for Fragrance

Alyssum maritimum
Asperula orientalis
Candytuft (Iberis)
Datura
Evening Primrose (Oenothera)
Exacum affine
Heliotrope
Limnanthes douglasii
Lupinus mutabilis
Mignonette (Reseda)
Nasturtium (Tropaeolum) Gleam varieties
Night-scented Stock (Matthiola bicornis)
Pansies (Viola)
Stocks (Matthiola)
Sweet Pea (Lathyrus odoratus)
Sweet Rocket (Lunaria)
Sweet Scabious (Scabiosa atropurpurea)
Sweet Sultan (Centaurea moschata)
Sweet William (Dianthus barbatus)
Tobacco (Nicotiana)
Verbena
Wallflower (Cheiranthus cheiri)

Index

251

258

NOTES

NOTES